A WISH BEYO

The Johnny Martino Story

A WISH BEYOND THE STARS

The Johnny Martino Story

BY

RICHARD LESTER

www.BookstandPublishing.com

Published by
Bookstand Publishing
Morgan Hill, CA 95037
3540_2

978-1-61863-098-8

Printed in the United States of America

Table of Contents

FOREWORD
By Johnny Martino

I have no doubt that I have lived my life my way. Over the years, I have met and worked with many of my childhood idols. I have friends in many places – from the underworld to the world of Hollywood -- and everywhere in-between.

I have enjoyed my singing and acting careers, as well as my jobs in restaurants, studio maintenance departments, and as an usher in a multiplex theatre. I may even have loved making a million manicottis in a pasta factory. If so, then I loved it all.

I thank my friends for the time that they have given me, and the patience they have needed in putting up with all of my craziness.

I am especially grateful to my childhood friend, Lucky Luciano, who always made sure I had butter on my pasta. Lucky also taught me that we are all related to each other in some way on this very small planet of ours. We are all human beings with a unique heart and soul.

I am deeply grateful to a very special friend named Al Pacino. Al has always been there for me, and our friendship stretches back more than 40 years.

I must also mention Mike Modor. Mike arranged for my first television job on *The Wild Wild West*. Because of his help, I was able to get my Screen Actors Guild card and realize my dream of making it big in Hollywood.

My appreciation list would not be complete without mentioning the father and son team of Richard and Gary Lester at Blue Heron International Pictures.

Gary is one of the finest directors I have ever worked with, and Richard has been amazing in turning my life story into print. I really love this book.

Finally, I am especially grateful for my family. God has been very good to me, and I have been richly blessed. To this day, I fondly recall my childhood days growing up with the best parents any child could ever hope for.

Top (L to R): Nicky, Jackie, Mimi, Mom, Dad, Tommy and Pete
Bottom (L to R): Charlie, Joey, Johnny

I love my brothers and sister, as well as my four beautiful daughters – Lisa, Cathy, Theresa, and Maria.

I am also very proud of my two wonderful sons -- Johnny and Joey. Johnny is currently in law school, while Joey is making good use of his economics education in both the sports and restaurant industries. I deeply love all of my children. They are among my richest of blessings.

Last -- but not least -- I must mention my loving wife, Lori. It was only through persistence that I was able to take this living angel as my bride, but I did it and we have spent the past twenty-five years together with our two sons. I will be thankful for Lori and all she has done for me until the day I die.

I love the special people who have come my way. I am amazed at all of the exciting things I have experienced over the past seven decades. My life was beautiful to begin with, and it hasn't changed in almost 75 years.

Yes, it is true that Paulie from *The Godfather* is now a senior citizen, but I wouldn't have it any other way.

I promise you that I will continue reaching for that dream beyond the stars and hoping to make our world a better place for all of our children and grand-children.

God love all of you, and thank you so much. You have helped make my dreams beyond the stars come true.

INTRODUCTION

"Leave the gun. Take the cannoli."

With those familiar words from Francis Ford Coppola's epic film, *The Godfather*, Marlon Brando's hit-men leave behind the bloody corpse of Paulie Gatto – played by actor Johnny Martino.

While Paulie was undoubtedly his most famous movie role, Johnny has spent considerable time portraying mobsters in such films as *Dillinger* and *Capone*. However, he actually started his show business career as a pop singer with Dick Clark back in the early days of television.

Yet, there is far more to Johnny Martino's story than can ever be imagined.

In *A Wish Beyond The Stars*, you will meet Johnny's large Italian immigrant family, along with Lucky Luciano, Pope Pius XII, Frank Sinatra, Marilyn Monroe, Marlon Brando, and John F. Kennedy.

You will travel to New York, Italy, and Hollywood -- visiting everything from movie sets and the Kefauver senate hearings to a neighborhood manicotti factory.

Johnny's story is like nothing you have ever read before. Leave the cannoli. Take the book. It is an offer you can't refuse.

Johnny and Lori Martino

1

THE EIGHTH SON

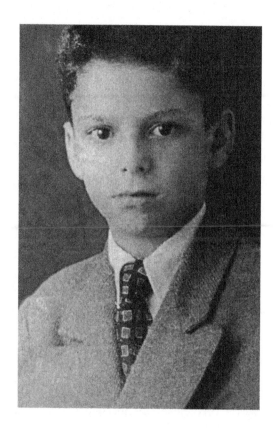

Gaetano Martino and Josephine Mignosi were born and raised in Palermo, Sicily. In search of a better life, they migrated to the United States at a young age.

The young immigrant couple brought an infant daughter to the New World with them, and every two years, they added a son to their family.

Seven sons later, Josephine wished beyond the stars that her ninth child would be a daughter. On May 05, 1937, Josephine gave birth to that ninth child -- her eighth son!

Johnny Martino came roaring into the world that day inside the family home in Brooklyn, New York. While she loved her new-born infant Giovanni, Josephine decided that no further effort would be made to add another daughter to the Martino family.

"I was born at 68 1st Place in Brooklyn," recalls Johnny (Giovanni). "My mother gave birth to every child at home with a midwife. It used to puzzle me. I used to say, 'Ma, you mean nobody was ever born in a hospital or anything?'

She said, 'No...You were all born at home.'

South Brooklyn was predominantly an Italian community back then. There were some Irish residents in the area, but it was a very close neighborhood with lots of people. We all knew each other.

When we moved to a Brownstone on Union Street, I remember thinking, 'Wow, I'm alive.' While I was growing up, I would frequently look up at the night sky and dream about the future. I would tell myself that I had a wish beyond those stars."

2

2

COMING TO AMERICA

"My father was only three years old when his father, Dominic Martino, passed away. My grandfather was in the Italian Navy stationed in Argentina. He had a fist fight with someone on the ship one day, and when he went home for lunch, he just keeled over and died of a heart attack. He was only 28 years old."

Johnny's grand-mother Rosalia then returned to Italy with her three year old child, Gaetano. A couple years passed, and the young Rosalia met a gentleman by the name of Veneziano, who had two children of his own from a previous marriage. Soon they were married, and Rosalia eventually had two daughters and another son.

Gaetano was around eight years old when his step-father wanted to adopt him and change his name. Johnny's dad somehow prevented the name change. He told his mother, "My father had no other children, and his name was Martino. I would like to keep the name Martino."

"My father kept his name," recalls Johnny proudly.

By 1914, the teenaged Gaetano told an uncle, "I wanna leave and go to America."

The uncle replied, "How you gonna go? You're too young. You really can't go."

"I do wanna go."

Finally, the uncle relented.

"You're gonna have to sneak on a ship, and that is how you can go. I can get you on board, but then you're on your own. You're only a little kid."

Gaetano didn't waiver. "Yeah I wanna do it."

The youngster from Palermo, Sicily soon found himself stowed away down the hatch of a freighter headed for New York.

"He thought America was the land of opportunity. His wish beyond the stars was to cross the ocean, come to this new land, and have a better life," recalls Johnny, who asked his father how long the voyage took.

Johnny's dad replied, "Well, I really don't know, but it was a very long time. It could have been 14 or 15 days." Johnny's curiosity about his dad's big adventure to the land of dreams had no limits.

"I asked him, 'What did you do for food all that time?'

He said, 'Well, all we had down in the hatch was lemons.'

I said, 'What?'

'We ate lemons.'

'You ate lemons all the time?'

'Yeah, we just had lemons.'

4

Can you imagine that? That's all they had to eat during the two week voyage to America."

***

Gaetano Martino finally arrived in New York City. After sneaking off the ship in the dark of night, he was surprised to see kids from other countries all scrambling around the docks also.

Gaetano spoke no English when he first set foot in America. However, his very survival depended on quickly learning how to communicate. It wasn't long before older men on the docks would pull him aside.

"Come here. Come here. You wanna make some money?"

Before long, Gaetano was loading and unloading trucks for 50 cents a day. Johnny asked him one day where he lived.

Gaetano replied, "Well there was a place called the baths. For 25 cents you could go for a bath and they gave you a cot. I did that for quite some time.

Then the next thing I know, I was getting smacked in the head a few times and shoved around. A couple Italian kids and I decided to stick together. We couldn't let them beat us up all the time. We needed to stick together."

At a young age, Gaetano Martino realized two important facts of life on the streets of New York.

First, you had to confront your adversary from a position of strength -- in numbers. Secondly, you had to be willing to resort to violence to protect what was yours. With this new knowledge, Gaetano started to fight back.

"We were tiny kids. We got together and started doing what we had to do to survive on the streets. We decided that we were not making enough money, so we thought maybe we could make a score here and there. We had to do little things like that to survive."

"By the time he was sixteen, my father got in trouble and they locked him up. He ended up going to jail. I said to him, 'So you went to jail?'

'Yeah I went to jail.'

I asked him for how long and he said two years."

3

AN OLD WORLD WEDDING

By the time Gaetano was 18, World War I had broken out. At that point, he got a lucky break. A corrections official called him in to an office and said, "Young man, you didn't do anything too bad. If you join the army, you could erase everything that happened."

It was an offer Gaetano could not refuse.

Before long, he was dressed in an American army uniform. Once again, he found himself on a ship crossing the Atlantic Ocean, but this time as an American soldier -- not a stowaway hiding in a hatch and subsisting on lemons.

Before he would return to his adopted country, Gaetano Martino would be wounded twice in battle – once in the leg and once in the wrist. When he did come home, he entered New York City as a newly minted American citizen.

Soon after, Gaetano was discharged from the army and wrote a letter to his mom in Italy. In the letter, he stated that he was coming back to Sicily to find a wife. Of course, this was exciting news for his mom, because she was going to get to see her son again.

Johnny Martino remembers his dad's account about what happened next.

"My father went back home to the same neighborhood where my mother lived. A family with eight children -- six sisters and two brothers – lived nearby. My father somehow made a choice between the girls and said, 'I like Josephine.'

He prepared to make a proposal. First, he talked to the family to see if they would grant permission for a marriage. Then, he had to determine if Josephine were interested in marrying him. Sure enough, it all worked out, and my father was about to become a married man."

The couple married in Italy on March 19th in a church named St. Rosalie. Johnny's sister was born in Italy, and the parents named her Rosalie, in honor of the church. The young couple stayed in Italy for eighteen months before Gaetano decided it was time to return to America with his new bride and daughter.

4

NEW YORK CITY

Back in New York, Johnny's father and mother began to have more children.

"My brother Mimi was the first Martino child born in America. Two years later, my brother Jackie came into the world. Then two years later, Mom gave birth to my brother Tommy. Two years after that, came my brother Petey, followed by my brother Joey. Two years later, my brother Nicky arrived. Then my brother Charlie was born. The Martino family was growing by leaps and bounds."

Fifteen months after Charlie was born, Johnny Martino came into the world -- the last of Gaetano and Josephine's children. It was 1937.

"The sleeping situation in that house was tight. There were four brothers in one bed, and two other brothers in another bed. My brothers Jackie and Mimi slept in another room separate from the rest of us.

There was also another bedroom for my sister. Of course my mom and dad were in a bedroom by themselves. With four brothers in a bed at night – all with their feet facing each other --

you just had to kick and fight for space. Then the older brothers in the other bed would yell out, 'Shut up and go to sleep.'

Fond memories now, but not so great back then."

***

As the 1930's gave way to the 1940's, America found itself once again at war. Johnny remembers living through World War II when he was five and six years old.

"We used to have air raid drills. The rule was that we had to shut off the lights. If you went out at that time, it was scary because I was told that sometimes they would throw sandbags out of a plane, and the sand bags would hit you.

As a kid, I do remember a thump on the roof one night. We immediately went up to the roof, and there we discovered a sandbag. It was made out of sack-like material with sand in it. There was some kind of print on the bag, but I can't remember what it said.

However, I do remember those days vividly. I recall one incident where I was outside playing with my brother Charlie, and there was a collie that lived down the block on Union Street.

One day I said, 'Charlie, the dog is loose,' and we began to run. I think that I was a little bit ahead of Charlie, but he was running pretty fast. I remember that the dog bit him. Then somebody yelled, and the dog ran off. He had bitten my brother on the leg. I think this was somewhere around 1942 or 1943.

I also remember an incident when I was four years old. My brother Charlie had been in the hospital and was sick. I went with my sister to see him, and I had a little toy with me.

We went into the hospital. Charlie was in a crib. He could have been maybe five or six years old at that time. He wanted the toy, and I remember him crying, saying that he wanted it. My sister told me to give the toy to Charlie because he was sick. I gave up the toy, but I wanted it back when we left.

***

Having so many brothers always made it fun around the house. I remember sitting at the dinner table with eleven people every day and again every night. My mother was about 5'1" and a beautiful little woman. My father was about 6'2" and weighed about 250 pounds. My mother cooked for everyone -- all the time.

***

My sister got out of school by the 7th grade to start working. She might have been about 12 years old. This was during the war, and she worked in a factory at that very young age.

My brother Mimi was a butcher and would work around the neighborhood as a kid. He was about nine years old -- scraping butcher blocks and learning how to cut meat. My brother Tommy followed suit, but Jackie ended up working on the waterfront when he got a little bit older.

11

At that time, my father worked as a superintendent on the waterfront. That's when I think I became acquainted with some of the people in the underworld.

My father became friends with Frank Costello, who eventually ended up the boss of New York's largest Mafia family. Of course, Lucky Luciano, the original boss of bosses, had been close friends with my father since their childhood days together in Sicily.

I did not know too much about Papa's life and the people that he hung out with. I didn't know them very well, because I was a little bit too young.

I did understand, however, that my brother Mimi caused some major excitement in our family right about this time."

5

MIMI ELOPES

"Every Sunday morning when I was around six years old, I listened to a radio program featuring singers competing with each other for a grand prize.

I remember one particular week when the grand prize winners were Frank Sinatra and Bing Crosby. My ten year old brother Jackie was a big Sinatra fan at that time. He would say, 'Johnny, listen. This is Frank Sinatra. He is a great singer. You're gonna like him a lot.'

That was all that I knew. I just kept hearing about Frank Sinatra.

During these early years of my life, there was a singer named Al Jolson, who was also very popular. I fell in love with his music. I would see little film clips of him in the movies, and I would think, 'What a great entertainer that guy is!' Al Jolson became my idol right along with Frank Sinatra. The year was 1943, and America was still at war.

My father was making trips back and forth to Italy, bringing American cigarettes to the soldiers. Penicillin had just been developed as a powerful antibiotic, and my father began 'importing' penicillin to Italy also.

"My brother Mimi was nineteen years old at the time, and I remember one day when I was in the kitchen. Mimi came

13

home and told me to come and give him a big hug. I asked him what he was doing, and he said, 'Come on, give me a kiss, give me a hug. I gotta go somewhere.'

I asked him where he was going, and he said that he was going away, and that he would be back in a few days. It was 1944. I must have been about seven years old.

I remember that my mother hugged Mimi and kissed him. Then he was gone. Where did he go?

He eloped with his girlfriend, Fanny!

I wondered why Mimi would elope. I soon learned that my father did not approve of the relationship. I am not sure what it was exactly, but Papa was not crazy about Mimi marrying that girl. Back then it was like that. Italian tradition.

Finally word got back to my father through Mimi's godfather. He was a guy named Joe who worked on the waterfront with my father. He was also a straightened-out guy – a member of one of the New York Mafia families.

Joe told my father, 'Hey listen. We all do things like that. The kid got married. You know you gotta forgive him.'

My father finally accepted this, and a huge crowd came over to the house for a reconciliation dinner.

The next thing you know, a year later, they had a baby -- my niece, Josephine. There was a whole big thing about having the first grand-child in the family -- a beautiful baby girl. My brother Mimi went on to have two more daughters."

***

Meanwhile, Johnny's father was making a number of trips to Italy. While Gaetano was away on one of those mysterious voyages, Josephine decided to move. She had an aunt who lived on Ocean Parkway in Brooklyn, who kept saying that she could buy a nice home and move in with the kids.

"My mother kind of brushed this off and stated that we had lived our entire lives in South Brooklyn, and that she was not going to leave. Her sister persisted, and asked her to come and take a look at a certain house.

We went to look at the place and it was beautiful -- four bedrooms, a huge living room, dining room, and a finished basement. It was a fantastic home, with an asking price of $11,000.

My father had put aside some extra money, and my mother decided to use some of it to buy the house. She paid cash. There was no mortgage.

Papa was still somewhere in Europe, possibly Italy. A great deal of secrecy surrounded every one of his trips.

By the time he came back to New York, we had already moved, and my father was a little bit upset not knowing where his family was. He knocked on the next door neighbor's house, and said, 'Angelina, where's my family?'

Angelina said, 'They moved. I will give you the address. They moved to Kings Highway.'

My father took down the address from the neighbor, and headed off to our new home. He was still a bit surprised when he arrived, and asked my mother to tell him all about it. Meanwhile, we were all happy because he was back home with us."

6

PETE JOINS THE NAVY

"As World War II dragged on, my brother Petey took one of my other brother's birth certificates and joined the Navy, not knowing what he was getting himself into. He was just a young teenager at the time.

My mother was in shock.

'How could my son do this?'

Mom called everyone she knew. They all told her the same thing -- Petey was too young, and the navy would send him back home.

'But he's already on the ship,' she wailed.

My brother had no idea where he was going. He told me that he really became nervous once he was on the ship and saw all the weapons. It was at that point that he realized he was in over his head."

Johnny's brother Pete approached one of the ship's non-commissioned officers.

"Listen, I gotta be honest. I made a mistake. I'm only fourteen years old."

The crew member had the perfect answer for the young sailor. He had Pete thrown in the brig, telling him that they would release him in four years when he turned eighteen!

Four years of confinement in a ship's brig was definitely not the way the teenager wanted to serve his tour in the U.S. Navy. He learned a few magic words, uttered them to the appropriate officials, and soon found himself released.

The next thing you know, Pete was doing some crazy things. He was given little assignments here and there on the warship. One of the work details consisted of painting the sides of the boat. Johnny still laughs when he tells the next part of his brother's story.

"He was out on a scaffold, painting the ship, hanging over the side. He said that he was out there with another young guy. He and the other sailor were kicking the plank and they were swinging on it, goofing around.

Suddenly, one of their kicks threw Pete off-balance and he fell overboard. He said that he sank underneath the ship, and did not remember anything after that. Apparently, he blacked out.

Fortunately, the other young sailor gave the 'man overboard' signal.

Pete told me that he woke up in sick bay and thought that he had died. He also mentioned something about the atomic bomb being transported. I think that he was a part of that mission."

18

Meanwhile, back home in New York, Johnny's mother kept going to the local churches in an effort to drum up support for Pete's release from the military.

There she would collect letters on behalf of her adventuresome fourteen year old son. She mailed letter after letter to the government, in an effort to get Pete out of the navy and bring him home.

It took two years before the government actually accepted that fact that they had a fourteen year old boy in uniform and assigned to a combat zone. The navy finally sent Josephine's adventurous son quietly back home, without the usual fanfare.

"Pete was a fun brother to be around," recalls Johnny. "We used to run in the snow together. I really missed him during the war. I love my brother Pete. I love all of my brothers. They all had different personalities. Every one of them was uniquely different."

Soon after the situation with Pete was resolved, Johnny's only sister Rosalie became engaged.

"She dated this guy, Jimmy," said Johnny. "They married and had three sons."

The Martino family continued to prosper and grow in America.

7

ADVENTURE IN SICILY

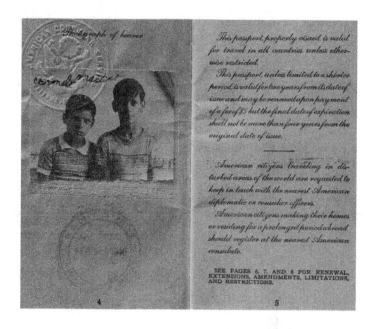

In 1947, with the war finally over, Gaetano Martino told his wife that it would be a good time for her to go to Italy to visit her family. She was apprehensive about the idea, especially when she thought about leaving some of the children behind.

Gaetano insisted that she go, however, as she had not seen her mother in more than 20 years. He told her she could take the two youngest boys – Charlie and Johnny.

Josephine then expressed concern about Nicky and Joey,

who were still young teenagers, but Gaetano reassured her -- reminding his wife that the visit was only expected to last for three months.

Gaetano then arranged for passports and the ocean passage, as well as care for the teen-aged children who would be left behind.

On a very cold February day in 1947, he and Josephine set sail for Italy, with Charlie and Johnny by their side. At the time, Josephine had no idea that her trip was a favor Gaetano was extending to the Number One Mafia crime boss in America – Lucky Luciano!

Johnny Martino had no idea of the real purpose of the trip either. As a ten year old, it seemed like quite an adventure.

"We went over on a medium-sized passenger ship. My father told me that I would get sea-sick and that the boat would rock a little bit.

He also told us that it was going to take a little time to get where we were going. We were in a first class cabin where there were beds for my mother and father. My brother and I were in bunk beds.

We set sail from New York harbor, and after a few hours, we did not see any more land. The boat was rocking a little bit, and Charlie and I started feeling a little woozy.

I asked Charlie if he felt alright, and he said that he was feeling a little dizzy and nauseous. My mother, brother, and I never left the cabin for two days after that. We spent the entire time nauseated and throwing up. We just could not adjust to the rocking of the boat.

Meanwhile, my father was constantly going to the dining room and bringing food back for us. Every time he brought us food, we would throw up again. It was crazy. After two days we started to feel a little bit more normal.

Finally, we were able to leave our cabin, look down the ship's corridors, and venture out to the dining room. We even started eating again. My brother and I started playing shuffleboard. We also would go to the game rooms where everybody played cards. We looked forward to four o'clock tea time. Our ocean voyage started to become a lot of fun.

After about two weeks at sea, we finally arrived in Genoa. I asked my father where we were. He told me that we were in northern Italy, and the ship would be dropping some of the passengers off, and picking some new ones up. Then, we would be sailing further south to Naples. My brother and I thought, 'OK, this is some voyage.'

We arrived in Naples, and were looking forward to getting off the ship. My brother and I only knew that we were going to visit our relatives in Sicily. We did not know about my Dad's load of two million dollars-worth of American cigarettes in the cargo hold – as well as the three cars -- two brand new Chryslers and a Pontiac – that were also on-board the ship with us."

As the Martino family stepped onto the dock, they were immediately surrounded by Italian plain-clothes detectives. Gaetano stepped away from his family to talk to the officers. Johnny remembers feeling apprehensive at this sudden turn of events, immediately after arriving in Italy.

"The next thing I know, my father says that he has to go with the men, and that he will be back. He told us that we would be taken care of, and we would go to the hotel there in Naples.

They soon took my father away. My mother, Charlie, and I were taken to a nice hotel in the heart of Naples. After a day, we received a notice that we could go and see my father. He had been put into some kind of prison facility.

When we went to see him, he was dressed the same. He still had on his expensive cashmere coat. The place looked like a really old type of prison.

Dad told us not to worry, and that he would be out in a couple of hours. Sure enough, he did get out. From what I understand, his bail was an outrageous amount – something like $200,000.

In Italy in 1947, that kind of bail was like a couple million dollars today. Dad must have had one heck of a cargo on that ship! No wonder he decided to escort it personally! In any event, someone appeared, and took care of the bail – all $200,000!

***

24

A very distinguished-looking gentleman named Giovanni came to see us. He knew that my father was coming to Sicily, and I was told he was a cousin of ours. Giovanni told us not to worry about anything. He assured us that my father would be out of prison almost immediately.

The next thing we knew, we were once again reunited on a boat going to Sicily. When you arrive in Sicily by boat, you are not exactly right in Palermo. You have to take a train. So at midnight, we found ourselves on a train.

My brother and I loved this two week adventure, even with the excitement caused by our arrival in Italy. After the train ride, we found a horse and wagon waiting for us. The driver of the wagon told us he would take us to my mother's family neighborhood.

We finally arrived in the wagon. My mother's family all turned out on the sidewalk to greet us. The neighborhood was still bombed-out from World War II. There were cobblestone streets, and everything was messy. There was a lot of rubble and destruction evident, with many buildings either completely or partially destroyed.

I remember saying to myself, 'Wow, what's going on? What are we doing here?" I thought that it was crazy for a ten year old kid to be looking at this devastation.

My brother and I did not know anybody standing there to welcome us. My father and mother, however, knew everyone. My mother had not seen any of her family -- sisters, brothers or mother -- for 23 years. Her father had died sometime earlier at 43 years old.

We got out of the wagon, and I remember that everyone was screaming with joy. There were lots of hugs and kisses. We went into the house to see my grandmother, who still wore an old-fashioned black mourning dress. In Sicily, they wear the black mourning outfit forever after someone passes away.

We went into the house, and the uncles and aunts were all hugging us and screaming with joy.

The shouting went on for at least an hour. There was a table full of food in the room. I could not believe how much food. I remember that it was very late at night -- close to 2:30 or 3:00 in the morning. Charlie and I were eating, but everyone else was still hugging and kissing.

My grandmother would not let go of my mother's hand. She was holding on to my mom for dear life.

My father teased her and told her to let my mother go, or he would take her back home right then.

My grandmother joked back at him in Italian, 'You ain't taking nobody. Get out of here. You took my daughter away from me all these years.'

Then, my mother made a major announcement to the entire group, which made my heart stop. She told them that I sing! Here I am, 10 years old, and she is telling them that her son sings – just like Al Jolson. I do not know if anyone there knew who Al Jolson was, but she told me to go ahead and sing like

26

him anyways. I got down on one knee and belted out his signature song.

Mammy, mammy,
The sun shines east, The sun shines west,
But I know where the sun shines best....
I'd walk a million miles for one of your smiles,
My mammy.

The crowd seemed to love every minute of it, even if it didn't remotely resemble any Italian love song that they may have been familiar with.

We spent that night at my grandmother's house. There was not much room because there were lots of people staying there with us.

So the next night, we headed off to a hotel in Palermo. I was about to meet the boss of bosses himself – Lucky Luciano!"

8

UNCLE CHARLIE

"The next day, my father left to arrange for the three cars and his other cargo to be off-loaded from the ship. After a few days at the hotel, my father told us that we were going to pick up someone who was a very good friend of his. He told us that he wanted us to call him 'Uncle Charlie' out of respect."

So at ten years old in Palermo, Italy, Johnny Martino met the first famous celebrity in his life – Charles 'Lucky' Luciano.

Little did he know that years later in Hollywood, he would also meet the most famous mob boss in movie history – the ultimate Godfather -- Marlon Brando.

In 1947, Johnny found it exciting enough to meet the real deal -- Lucky Luciano.

"I remember that we were in my father's burgundy Pontiac. One of the Chryslers was for Lucky Luciano. The other one was for Joe Adonis.

Out of nowhere, Lucky appears and gets into our car. Of course there is a big hug and a kiss between him and my dad, followed by smiles and hand-shaking. I learned later that he and Lucky had been close friends ever since their childhood days in Sicily.

My father introduced us to Uncle Charlie Luciano, who asked us, 'How are you kids?'

Lucky then asked if we would do him a favor, and we said, 'Okay.' He told us, 'As long as you're in my company, speak only English, because I really miss America.'

From that moment on, all we did was talk in English with him. Lucky told us stories about New York. He said that he loved New York and missed that city very much. He did not go into detail about who he was. All I knew was that he was a perfect gentleman, a very, very nice person.

A lot of people wondered where the name Luciano came from. In Italian, it is a first name, the same as Martino. I never knew that Martino was meant to be a first name. For a boy, the name would be Martino, and for a girl it would be Martina.

I found out that 'Lucky' became Uncle Charlie's nickname because he gambled quite a bit, and won most of the time. I found this out years later. At that time, Uncle Charlie was simply a lot of fun to be around.

After picking up Uncle Charlie, we went to the hotel where he had his own room. I believe that there was a young lady there waiting for him. She had been a friend of his for many, many years.

She was a very beautiful woman with black hair. I remember her very distinctly. She had been with him during his years in New York, and now they were together in Italy.

Uncle Charlie checked into his room, and we went back to our own room with our mother. I remember that my father said that Uncle Charlie wanted to see us in his room. So my brother and I walked over and knocked on his door. We heard him invite us in.

Charlie and I went in, and I remember that Lucky Luciano was actually enjoying the fact that we were two little American boys speaking to him in English.

We were in the room, and I remember that he had some luggage. He had a suitcase on the bed and he had opened it up. It was a suitcase full of ties!

Lucky was going through the suitcase, and a moment later he took out two ties. In the 1940's, a knitted tie was extremely popular. He told me that we might be too young to wear them, but that our father might wear them for the time being.

He told us to hold on to them, and that someday we would say, 'Wow! Lucky Luciano gave me these ties.'

I still have those ties to this day. They meant so much to me at that time, and still do. When my father passed away, the ties were still in his closet.

At that time I thought about the ties and how they were given to us, and that I needed to keep them. So I did. I have treasured those little friendship gifts from my childhood friend, Lucky Luciano, ever since."

***

Johnny Martino's memories of the childhood trip to Sicily are filled with many happy moments shared with relatives from both sides of his family, including his two grandmothers.

However, ten year olds soon get bored with family visits. It wasn't long before Uncle Charlie saved the day.

Uncle Charlie Luciano and friend

"To pass the time for me and my brother while we were in Italy, I remember that Lucky Luciano had said that he would do something with us.

He asked us if we liked horses, and of course we said yes. He told us that he was going to buy a horse and wagon, and that he would make arrangements with someone he trusted to take us around town. He spared no expense in showing me and my brother a good time.

Uncle Charlie's 'employee' took us everywhere. He even took us to the beach. The ocean was amazing. You could walk out on the sand for at least 100 to 200 feet, and the water would still only be up to your knees.

We were royally entertained by this guy with the horse and wagon. He would take us to the track where they had the trotters, and he would drive us around in the little double wagon.

He would have us sit up next to him and then get the horse running. I remember looking at the ground and seeing how fast the horse was going. I just loved this.

I can also remember going where they had actual racing, and Lucky would take us at night. The whole family would go. Lucky would ask me what number I wanted, and I would tell him that number eight was my lucky number. He would place the bet for us and give us the ticket.

I remember we had great times in restaurants, and everywhere we went in Italy. It was a childhood dream come true!"

***

Johnny Martino's childhood adventure in post-war Italy also included cultural opportunities which he never knew existed. At ten years old, he was introduced to the European ballet. Seated in the theatre that night were his mother, father, brother -- and Lucky Luciano with his long-time female companion.

After the performance, Lucky confided in Johnny's mother that he was attracted to one of the ballerinas performing on-stage that night.

He whispered to Josephine that he wanted to send the young dancer some flowers and ask her for a date. Johnny learned the details afterwards from his mother.

"My mother explained to us that Lucky wanted to go out with this other girl, a very nice person and a great dancer. Lucky had asked my mother if she could approach the performer, (whose name was Igea Lissoni), and see if she would consent to a double date with him and my parents.

At that time, Lucky was about 49 and Igea was 24. My mother did approach the young lady. Somehow, Mom arranged to see her backstage.

Mom actually talked the attractive dancer into going on a double date with Lucky Luciano. She told her not to worry, and not to believe everything that she read or heard about him.

It was an offer Igea couldn't refuse. They all went out on a double date. Before long, Igea discovered that she really liked Lucky Luciano.

Igea was from a well-to-do and very nice family from Milan. She was a little bit nervous about the possibility of upsetting her family, because she was going with someone who was not only very charismatic, but also somewhat notorious.

As it turned out, Lucky and Igea did date for quite some time, and we had almost a family relationship with her as well. As time went on, she drew closer to me and my brother. She was just the sweetest thing in the world. We loved her so much."

Months later, the Martino family still found themselves living a life of ease in Italy. Gaetano continued to be out on bail, awaiting trial. Johnny and his brother Charlie were becoming real Italians, fluent in the language, and familiar with various dialects and customs.

Then one day, Johnny discovered that he would be making a very special trip to Rome.

9

THE POPE

"We went to Rome and my father told my brother Charlie that he should ask Lucky Luciano to be his godfather at his confirmation. So Charlie said sure, that he would ask him.

We went out to dinner and my father told Lucky that my brother wanted to say something to him. We were sitting in a restaurant in Rome, and my brother said, 'Uncle Charlie, I would like to ask you to be my sponsor -- to be my godfather -- at my confirmation.'

Lucky said, 'Oh my God, I love it.'

I remember that Lucky got up and hugged my brother. He told him, 'Oh yes, definitely. We'll do it as soon as we get back to Sicily.'

This was a big moment for my brother. It was obviously a big moment for Lucky Luciano also."

It was a big moment for Johnny Martino, as well. Lucky Luciano was the first godfather he would meet, but he would not be the last. Twenty-five years later, Johnny would find himself close by Marlon Brando's side -- a member of Hollywood's Corleone family, in Francis Ford Coppola's epic film – *The Godfather*.

***

"When I was a ten year old in Rome, I wasn't too impressed with some of the city's finest restaurants. I remember being fussy about the sauce on the macaroni. It was too thick, and I did not like the taste of the red sauce.

After agreeing to be my brother's godfather, Lucky Luciano turned to me and asked me what I would like to eat, since I did not like the food in front of me.

I told him that maybe I would like some macaroni with butter. My mother chimed in and said that I would really like that.

38

Lucky called the waiter over and told him to bring me macaroni with butter, along with some chicken broth and extra parmesan cheese. In subsequent visits, he arranged for the restaurant to prepare my food the way I liked it each time we dined there.

That particular day, Lucky turned to me and said that he wanted to ask me a question. He picked up a regular butter knife and asked, 'What if I cut my finger? What happens?'

I told him that he would bleed.

He said, 'Yeah that's right. I would bleed.'

I started wondering what this was all about.

Lucky then asked me what would happen if he cut *my* finger.

I told him that I would bleed too.

"Remember what I just told you,' said Lucky Luciano. 'Do you know what it means?

I told him that it meant that everybody bleeds. He told me never to forget this.

'Everybody bleeds.'

I thought about this conversation my whole life, and have come to believe that Lucky's message was that we are all very closely related. We are all human beings, and we all have a heart that beats. I have never forgotten his words to me through all the years. He told me, 'You know we're all the same. We are all people. We all bleed.'

To me, Lucky Luciano was not an evil mob boss. He was a compassionate human being. Most important of all, he was my childhood friend."

***

"We spent a lot of time that year with my mother's family, as well as my father's family -- and Lucky Luciano. We experienced a lot of really wonderful things in Italy, but perhaps the best was saved for last.

When Charlie asked Lucky Luciano to be his godfather, it touched Lucky's heart. He was excited about doing this. Lucky had never been married. He had never had children. He felt like Charlie and I were his children at that point. The two of us were constantly around him that entire year.

I remember one day when we were having dinner at someone's home in Rome. We arrived at a beautiful building that had been completely untouched by the war.

We entered the building and were ushered up to the penthouse. There we met our host. It was Giovanni, the heavyset gentleman with a pleasant personality and thin, gray hair. Giovanni spoke beautiful Italian.

As we sat down for dinner, I noticed that he had an oriental chime at the table. Giovanni hit the chime and the servants entered the room to serve us. It was pretty impressive stuff for a ten year old kid from Brooklyn.

Lucky Luciano had already spoken to Giovanni about Charlie's confirmation ceremony. Apparently, Giovanni had some pretty good connections at the Vatican.

The day after our dinner at Giovanni's palatial home, we went to the Vatican. There, we were greeted by several of the staff members who worked directly with the Pope.

They soon ushered us into a private room. I remember before we went into the room that they explained to us that the Pope was there and he was waiting to see us.

I now realize how much clout Lucky's friend Giovanni must have had with the Vatican to be able to set up a personal meeting for us with the Pope.

The Vatican staff members opened the doors and we went into the room. Pope Pius XII was sitting there. I recognized him instantly because of his round glasses.

Pope Pius softly told us to come closer. My mother whispered into my ear to just kiss his hand. My brother and I stepped up to the Pope, wide-eyed and speechless.

The Pope patted each of us on the head, and we kissed his hand. Then, he saw Lucky Luciano and made a gesture for Lucky to come closer.

I can still picture the scene in my mind. There we were -- Lucky, Giovanni, my mother, father, brother and me in the same room with Pope Pius XII. In the Vatican! In Rome! In Italy! If only the neighborhood kids could see me now!

The next few days we enjoyed the sights in Rome. We went to the races, ate at nice restaurants, and really had a wonderful time before returning to Sicily.

Then the day of Charlie's confirmation arrived.

We all stood in a round circle inside the church with other children waiting to be confirmed. They seemed to be from all different countries.

Charlie was standing there with Lucky Luciano.

My mother, father and I -- along with Igea Lissoni (who had become Lucky's constant companion) -- were all standing within the group. Charlie then received the sacrament of confirmation from the Catholic Church, with Lucky Luciano standing in as his godfather.

It was a tradition in the Catholic faith for the godfather to give the godson a watch. Lucky gave Charlie a very nice gold watch. I remember thinking that my brother received a wonderful confirmation present. What I didn't know, was that Lucky had also arranged a little surprise for me.

When we arrived back at the hotel, Igea asked me to sit next to her. She was really beautiful. I just loved her. She looked like Ingrid Bergman. Whenever I watch the movie *Casablanca* and see Ingrid Bergman on screen, I think of Igea. Even though I was only ten years old, I knew beyond any doubt that she was a sweet and beautiful person, full of love.

As I sat next to Igea, she handed me a gold watch. My fingers were shaking as I examined my special gift. The watch

42

was made of platinum gold with yellow gold handles. I knew who the watch came from. Lucky Luciano always treated both me and my brother equally. Charlie gets a watch for his confirmation. Johnny gets one too.

Both watches no longer exist today. Years later, my brother Tommy borrowed my gold watch to go on a date. Before the night was over, Tommy ended up in a fist-fight, and the watch was destroyed during the melee.

Later in life, my brother Charlie's four year old son found his special watch. While playing with it, the child decided to see what would happen if he flushed it down the toilet."

***

The gold watch Lucky Luciano gave to Johnny's mother

10

ARRIVIDERCI, PALERMO

Shortly after Charlie's confirmation, the Martino-Luciano group prepared to say their goodbyes. It was time for Johnny and his family to head back home to America.

To the Martinos, it was very obvious that Lucky Luciano had fallen deeply in love with Igea. Luciano was a man who always remembered the people who were good to him, and he was very much aware of the role Johnny's mother played in bringing Igea into his life.

Johnny was there the night Lucky Luciano expressed his appreciation.

"I was at home with my brother. The adults were out late and my aunt was babysitting us. Since we ended up staying in Italy much longer than we originally planned, my father had rented a nice apartment.

My mother and father came home around 10 PM. That night Lucky Luciano had given my mother a beautiful watch. He told her, 'This is for you, Josie -- for what you did for the love of my life.'

I have often thought about the watch that Lucky Luciano gave to my mother. It is the only Luciano watch that has survived the passage of time, and it remains in my possession today."

After a year of excitement, adventure, and pure fun for Johnny and his brother Charlie, it was finally time for the Martino family to head back to New York.

The boys found it difficult to say their goodbyes to Lucky and Igea, who were also emotionally choked up at seeing their adopted family heading back home to a country that Lucky could never enter again.

"I remember everyone in tears," recalls Johnny.

"I remember distinctly that Lucky Luciano said to my mother, 'You have eight sons, you can leave two.'

My mother laughed and said, 'Well I do, but I love them all the same. I can't give up the boys.'

Igea kept hugging us and telling us in Italian that she loved us so much. It was so sad.

Lucky Luciano told us, 'I love you. You're like my sons. You gotta come back. Okay? I'm gonna wait for you. You come back when you're 18 years old. Now give me a hug.'

I hugged Lucky Luciano one more time, and my brother hugged him too. Then it was time to leave.

The man from Rome – Giovanni -- was there also. He adored our family too. He was such a nice man. He told us that he was going to come to New York on the ship with us.
46

On the ship, my mother told me, 'Giovanni could be *your* godfather.' I was about 10 at the time, which was the winter of 1948.

I did ask Giovanni to be my godfather. He seemed delighted, hugging me and telling me we shared the same first name.

We arrived in New York and were getting off the ship. I said to my father, 'Where's my godfather?'

He said, 'Something happened and he has to go back to Italy.'

It turned out that the customs officials would not even let Giovanni off the ship. I'm thinking, 'What did he do? Did he have to go back and see the Pope?'

My father told me not to worry about it, and that we would get someone else."

11

THE KEFAUVER SHOW

At ten years old, I had no idea who Lucky Luciano really was. I could never even begin to imagine that this kind and gentle man who treated me and my brother as if we were his own children could possibly be the boss of bosses in New York at that very same time.

I found out years later that Lucky Luciano had supposedly formed the five New York Mafia families, and even coined the phrase 'boss of bosses.'

It was just overwhelming to me to even contemplate that, after spending so much time with him. He was just another human being, as nice as he could be to me and my brother.

We never saw any temper. We never saw the man angry, upset, or impatient with us. We always saw him as such a pleasant and caring person. He was the source of immense childhood joy during our year in Italy.

I often wondered about Lucky's reputation. Was it really deserved? If Lucky Luciano was such a major mobster, how come he was never charged with murder, or robbery, or interstate crime, or narcotics violations – crimes a major mobster would be expected to commit?

Yet, New York Prosecutor Thomas E. Dewey, on his way to a national political career, was only able to charge Lucky and convict him for abetting prostitution. *Abetting prostitution!* What type of penalty would that type of offense receive today?

Back then, it got Lucky a 30 year sentence at Dannemora."

Thomas E. Dewey wasn't the only politician who hoped to climb to fame as a crime-buster. Tennessee Senator Estes Kefauver also saw an opportunity to advance his political fortunes using crime as the platform as well.

Kefauver initially had his sights on the chairmanship of the House Un-American Activities Committee. However, when the Republican leadership in Congress gave that plum assignment to Joe McCarthy – the junior senator from Wisconsin who had a serious alcohol problem -- Kefauver decided that the chairmanship of the Senate Committee on Organized Crime in Interstate Commerce was better than nothing.

The wily senator knew how to create a political circus. He turned his consolation prize into a media spectacle that few could ever have imagined.

By the time the Kefauver Crusade was over, millions of Americans had watched the committee hearings on television, and the committee actually traveled to 14 cities to root out crime and corruption in America.   Interestingly, the show never travelled to Tennessee, Kefauver's home state and political base. Memphis bookmakers had escaped the national Kefauver dragnet.

New York crime boss Frank Costello did not escape, however. From March 13 until March 30, 1951, those Americans who owned television sets became addicted to America's first reality television show. Opening guest star was none other than Frank Costello.

Families would gather around the TV sets, eating TV dinners, and listening to Frank's gravelly voice repeat one line over and over: "On advice of counsel, I decline to answer on the grounds that it may incriminate me.'

***

Frank Costello's voice also fascinated Marlon Brando. Years later, he would imitate that same voice in his portrayal of Don Corleone in *The Godfather*.

The Kefauver hearings certainly influenced the Martino family's television viewing habits. When Joe Adonis was called to testify, Johnny wondered if he would mention the cars that his father brought to Italy for Joe and Lucky Luciano back in 1947. Joe Adonis, however, wasn't giving up any more than Frank Costello did.

"I likes ya," Adonis told the committee. "Youse can call me Joey A."

After that, he too declined to answer any committee questions.

Then the shock of shocks occurred for the Martino family. Johnny's father received a subpoena to also testify on television before the Kefauver Committee.

While all three television networks (NBC, CBS, and ABC) carried live coverage of the hearings daily, none of them had an actual production crew in place. The cameras and crew all belonged to New York's Channel 11 – WPIX – the same outfit that broadcast a charity event boxing match featuring young Johnny Martino two years earlier!

Now his own father would have a guest star appearance on America's first television reality show, which was attracting audiences in excess of 30 million people each day.

As Johnny likes to point out, both he and his father were brought before television audiences by the same New York TV station -- WPIX. How ironic is that?

52

The Kefauver Committee took an interest in Lucky Luciano, despite the fact that he had never been arrested or convicted of any organized crimes involving interstate commerce. Nevertheless, every drama needs a villain, and casting director Estes Kefauver felt that Lucky Luciano was perfect for the part.

Decades later, the United States government began declassifying naval intelligence documents from World War II.

In this unlikeliest of settings, Lucky Luciano again popped up in a starring role – this time as the hero, not the villain. Johnny Martino could not believe his eyes, when he began reading through the files.

"Imagine my shock when I discovered recently that there was yet another side to Lucky Luciano -- a side that he kept secret, a side that ultimately saved thousands of American lives in World War II.

Lucky Luciano was far more than a gangster. My father was right by his side during the war, and now that story can finally be told."

12

LUCKY GOES TO WAR

Lucky Luciano relaxing at home

Salvatore Lucania was born in Sicily in 1897. Sixty-five years later, he died in Sicily.

Salvatore was raised in poverty, but died a very wealthy man. Although he never became a citizen, he deeply loved America. However, America did not love him. To the politicians, Salvatore Lucania was Lucky Luciano, the father of organized crime in America.

There is no disputing the fact that Lucky Luciano was the main force behind the creation of New York's five major Mafia families. There is no doubt that his underworld business enterprises made him a very wealthy man.

However, Lucky Luciano was a very intelligent person, whose business instincts never failed him. He could have easily made his millions legally.

In fact, less than a month before he collapsed from a fatal heart attack at Naples' Capodichino Airport in 1962, Luciano told reporters, "I learned too late that you need just as good a brain to make a crooked million as an honest million. These days, you apply for a license to steal from the public. If I had my time again. I'd make sure I got that license first. I'd do it legal."

However, in 1936, Lucky Luciano was not 'doing it legal.' On May 11, 1936, he went on trial on the prostitution charges. The principal witness against him – Cokey Flo Brown – was a streetwalker and prostitute withdrawing from a heroin addiction at the time.

Lucky's attorneys believed she would say anything to please the prosecutors and get what she needed to come off the addiction. One of Lucky's friends felt the prosecution was mounted against his name and reputation, and had little to do with the facts of any alleged crimes.

To top it all off, Cokey Flo repudiated her testimony after the trail. She made it clear that none of what she had testified to in court was true.

Nevertheless, prosecutor Thomas E. Dewey knew the success of his political career rested on Lucky going to prison and staying in prison. When the trial was over, the judge buried Lucky Luciano. He was sentenced to thirty to fifty years in state prison for abetting prostitution.

When Japanese war-planes flew into Pearl Harbor in 1941, Lucky Luciano was working in the prison laundry at Dannemora. He had no idea that his luck was about to change, and his adopted country was about to have a change of heart regarding his future.

***

There are some historians today who believe that Lucky Luciano was deprived of a fair trial and appropriate punishment. The prosecution made no effort to hide the fact that they wanted a conviction based as much on his reputation as on the alleged facts of the crimes. In the end, Lucky was sentenced to an unprecedented term merely on prostitution-related charges.

At the same time, war clouds were moving in over Europe, and German Jews were beginning to suffer under Nazi tyranny. The worsening conditions for European Jews did not escape the attention of Jewish mobster Meyer Lansky.

In July, 1933, shortly after Hitler became Chancellor of Germany, the German-American Bund was created in the United

States. Major centers were set up in Milwaukee, Los Angeles, and New York City – Lansky's home turf.

Five years later, at the annual Columbus Day Parade, Italian Fascists cheered Mussolini, but ignored Mayor Fiorello LaGuardia. Lansky's concerns deepened.

With the German-American Bund approaching a staggering membership of 250,000 members -- many of whom were staging marches in their Storm Trooper uniforms -- Lansky decided to act.

"My friends and I saw good action against the Brown Shirts. I got my buddies like Bugsy Siegel. We didn't behave like gents."

Lansky's rise to the top in the American underworld was financed in part by several wealthy members of the Jewish establishment, who saw Lansky and his crew as a counter-force to the home-grown Nazis. Hitler's surrogates in New York City began to pay a price in broken bones, bloody noses, assorted bruises, and black eyes.

On December 7, 1941, the Japanese attacked Pearl Harbor. America declared war on Japan. Germany declared war on America. Italy had no recourse but to follow Germany's lead. World events had drastically shaken up the lives of Germans, Italians, and native-born Americans in New York City.

A volatile mix of people from various ethnic backgrounds lived and worked in New York City, which was America's most strategic port. The United States government
58

immediately recognized how vulnerable that port could be to enemy sabotage.

New York City offered 80 miles of coastal footage containing 200 cargo docks, warehouses, piers, and countless businesses connected with shipping, fishing, and world trade.

Government experts also remembered that during World War 1, the waterfront had been completely infiltrated by enemy agents.

So it is no surprise today to learn that a high profile underworld delegation set out for Dannemora Penitentiary only days after the attack on Pearl Harbor.

There is no evidence of any direct involvement on the part of the United States government at that point in time, but the fact is that underworld chieftain Meyer Lansky and top New York mobster Frank Costello were welcomed with open arms by prison officials, who arranged for them to meet privately with inmate Lucky Luciano.

"What are the odds of something like that happening without some influence from the highest levels of government?" asks Johnny Martino.

In any event, Lansky and Costello left the prison with a secret plan in place devised by Lucky Luciano. That deal with the United States government has been outlined in detail in the Herlands Report of 1954.

Incredibly, the report remains unpublished to this day. In it, Lucky Luciano outlines a protection plan for New York's docks that was undeniably successful.   Initially,   Luciano arranged with New York's Mafia captains to provide fisherman's union cards to undercover naval intelligence agents.

The union cards allowed the government to have eyes and ears on many of the larger fishing boats coming in and out of New York harbor. Hanging around the docks and working on the boats, undercover government agents would be in a position to gather solid intelligence about German submarine activity in the area -- including their re-supply lines, which everyone knew extended into the city.

So naval intelligence went to war in New York City equipped with credentials and cover supplied by the Mafia.

Agents quickly learned not to share their suspicions about possible enemy agents with their underworld collaborators, however. The few times that they did, those suspected enemy agents quickly and mysteriously disappeared, probably with concrete blocks tied to their feet before being dumped in the New York harbor.

Since the government preferred enemy agents alive and able to be questioned, naval supervisors quickly learned to keep some things secret from their dockside partners.

Luciano's protection plan was working so well, that on May 12, 1942, he was transferred out of the grim maximum security facility of Dannemora to the much more pleasant environment found at Great Meadow prison.

The transfer also brought Luciano closer to New York City, allowing government agents more time and easier access to deal with him directly.

It seems ironic that during World War II, Lucky Luciano was running the mob's biggest protection racket from inside a prison -- aided and abetted by the United States government.

At this time in American history, the Mafia was so powerful on the New York docks, that Lucky was able to make a bold promise to the naval intelligence agents involved with the protection program.

"Every individual who has anything to do with the coming and going of ships to the United States," said Lucky, "is now helping the fight against the Nazis."

Maybe not quite everybody.

On January 9, 1942 a fire broke out on the New York City waterfront. Then a month later, at 2:30 AM on February 9, 1942, the newly converted troop ship Normandie was set ablaze at Pier 88.

When the fires were finally extinguished, the ship had sustained substantial water damage from fire-fighting efforts. The 55 million dollar warship ended up transporting no troops to Europe. It was eventually sold for scrap.

Less than two months after Hitler vowed to strike first, one of America's largest naval vessels was destroyed right in New York harbor, which was under the personal protection of Lucky Luciano.

Incredibly, the government did not see the loss of the Normandie as an exception to Luciano's highly successful protection plan. Allowing the public to think it was the work of German saboteurs may have been great propaganda, but it was far from the truth.

Working closely with the mob, investigators discovered that the fire was accidentally set by a workman who got careless with a blow-torch. He summoned assistance, and fire-fighters arrived in plenty of time to save the ship.

However, they indiscriminately let loose with their water cannons, and inadvertently caused the ship to list and eventually sink. The Normandie went down not because of Nazi saboteurs, but at the hands of patriotic – and very careless – Americans!

By 1943, it was obvious that Lucky Luciano had kept his side of the bargain. The government, however, was faced with a dilemma. If they pardoned him, Lucky would immediately be deported – to Mussolini's Italy.

The Washington bureaucrats came up with a plan worthy of any Mafia godfather. They convinced Lucky Luciano to stay in jail!

At this point, Luciano had delivered his part of the bargain, and the government negotiated to postpone making good on their end. If Lucky would agree to stay as an inmate at Great Meadow, and continue to help with the war effort, the government was prepared to go to the very top in Washington at the end of the war and seek executive clemency for him.

Everybody knew what that meant. The President himself would become involved. Lucky would be released from prison at the end of the war and not be deported. It was an offer he could not refuse.

As the Germans were beginning to retreat from North Africa, America's military planners started looking at an invasion of Europe -- possibly through Italy. Luciano suggested that allied forces land near Palermo in Sicily, the home of many powerful Italian Mafiosi whom he and Gaetano Martino knew personally.

The Americans agreed, and Lucky set into motion a plan to make contact with the mob in Nazi-occupied Sicily. In the course of this plan, Luciano laid the groundwork for a successful Allied landing with a minimum of American casualties. There is no doubt that his efforts saved hundreds – if not thousands – of American GIs on the initial invasion of Europe.

On July 9, America launched Operation Husky and the citizens of Palermo – including the powerful Sicilian mob bosses -- were the first to be freed from the Nazis. There is a report in folklore that the initial American tanks to roll into that area flew green banners with the letter L on them – indicating they were part of Luciano's secret pact with the Sicilian mob bosses. American intelligence agents reported that, "Luciano's information was also of tremendous help following the landing."

Perhaps the Herlands Report of 1954 sums up best Lucky Luciano's contribution to the successful war effort at home and abroad:

"Luciano and his associates and contacts – during a period when the outcome of the war appeared extremely grim – were responsible for a wide range of services which were considered useful to the Navy."

***

On January 3, 1946, former prosecutor – and now New York governor – Thomas E. Dewey commuted Lucky Luciano's prison sentence to time served.

Perhaps because he was about to become a candidate for president of the United States, he did little else on Lucky Luciano's behalf.

President Harry Truman also saw no reason to honor an understanding made on behalf of his predecessor in the Oval Office with representatives of navy Lt. Commander Charles Haffenden.

So, on February 9, 1946, the United States government reneged on its promise of executive clemency. On behalf of a grateful nation, they deported Lucky Luciano to Sicily instead.

***

13

JOHN CASSAVETES

John Cassavetes

Back in New York after a year's vacation in Italy, Johnny wasted little time getting back in the groove.   Before he left home in 1947, the principal at PS 97, asked Johnny's mother to bring her back a cameo pin from Italy. She did, but by the time the family returned, the principal had passed away. The cameo pin ended up staying in the Martino family.

"My mother kept it all of those years," said Johnny.

Since he had missed a year of school, Johnny was placed back in the fourth grade. He had no problem with that.

"It was okay because I had met the kids that were in the grade below me and I became very good friends with a guy named Joey. We became the best of friends during that year. We are still friends today. That whole situation worked out fine."

Johnny admits that he did not set any world records while in elementary school, however.

"I have to be honest. I was not the greatest student in the world. I was okay. If I took a spelling test, I had to study really hard to get a 100.

I was pretty good with math. I never read well, however. I guess I did not have an interest.

My brother Jackie was a teenager working on the waterfront. Since my father had been a big-time boss on the waterfront back in the 1930's, Jackie had no trouble finding work. My mother had mentioned that when I was born they had a lot of money. We were comfortable in life.

My brother Joey was working at the time in a gas station, learning to become a mechanic. Joey was also a teenager. He was five years older than me and working at the local Texaco station.

I remember one day that he did not go in. He didn't feel good. He told my brother Charlie to go into the gas station and take his place. Charlie said, 'I'm only 13 years old.'

Joey told him, 'You can do it.'

Charlie reported to the gas station and learned how to pump gas and fix a flat tire. I think that on that day, his life changed forever. He decided to become a mechanic and wanted to work in gas stations his whole life.

As he grew up, Charlie started to own the gas stations. He became a very good mechanic. That day when Joey became too sick to go to work changed Charlie's life forever. Eventually, Charlie also went to work for the New York City Board of Education, overseeing their transportation department.

Cars and part-time work were also becoming a part of my life. There was a used car lot a few blocks away, and I applied for a job there. I might have been twelve at the time. I don't remember exactly. I used to clean and wipe down the cars after school.

The nice guy who owned the lot was named Mimi, like my brother. One weekend, I was cleaning the cars and noticed that he didn't come in to work. On Monday after school, I reported for duty and Mimi still wasn't there.

Carroll Nash, the salesman, came up to me. He said, 'John, we're closed today.'

I asked him, 'Why? Why are we closed?'

Mr. Nash told me that Mimi had flown somewhere, the plane crashed, and he died. I could not believe this. Mimi could not have been more than 40 years old, and he was a very nice looking guy. Yet, there it was. He died in a plane crash.

I went back a couple of days later, and Mr. Nash was still there. He told me that I could stay on.

I remember cleaning the cars. In those days, the cars were big. I used to clean the roofs standing on a milk box. I would put the milk box alongside the vehicle, climb up, and wipe the roofs down with a towel.

The cars were different colors, but most of them were black. They would streak if you did not wipe them down just right. Anyway, for my very first job, I cleaned cars."

Cleaning cars was not part of young Johnny Martino's dream. While singing and acting were his priority career goals, he ended up appearing on television for the first time in a most unexpected way.

"I was twelve years old in 1949 and doing a little boxing on the side. Somehow my name got submitted during a citywide search to fight at the Broadway Arena in a benefit event for the war veterans. I was chosen to fight an Irish kid by the name of Tommy Kelly.

Imagine my surprise when I learned that we would be on the same card that night as Jake LaMotta – the Raging Bull himself!

I remember sitting in the dressing room in my robe and trunks and gloves, feeling a little nervous. The event was to be telecast by WPIX television – Channel 11. I was going to box in front of a New York City television audience as well as live for the boxing fans in the arena.

Suddenly, my thoughts were interrupted, as none other than Jake LaMotta comes strolling into the dressing room.

'Whadda you doin' here, Kid?'

'I'm boxing tonight.'

'Boxing?'

'Yeah.'

'You got medical insurance?

As he left the room, the Raging Bull parted with, 'Take care of yourself, Kid.'

That night, I returned home with a massive headache, assorted bruises, and a ten dollar gift card to a local department store. I decided then and there that the next time I was on television, it wouldn't be as a boxer."

***

As the decade of the 1940's transitioned into the Fabulous Fifties, exciting things began happening in the pop music world. Johnny started to develop an interest beyond cleaning cars and boxing.

"I would try to sing all the time, even at home. Wherever I was, I would sing. I decided I wanted to take singing lessons. I didn't know where to go, or where to start. My brothers worked in butcher shops, as mechanics in garages, or on the waterfront. None of them were the least bit interested in a singing career.

I had a friend named Charlie Padula. He was another guy I grew up with, and he was also close to my best friend, Joey. The three of us guys hung out a lot together.

One day, I said to Charlie, 'Let's go to New York City.' I think the year was 1953 and I was about 16. So, we headed into Manhattan.

We went to all the local places, and I checked to see if there were anywhere I could get singing lessons. I would get a lead about this place or that place, but nothing was panning out.

The next thing I knew, this guy told me about a black lady named Leola Carter, who taught singing lessons. She was on Seventh Avenue around 53rd Street.

I soon located Leola in her little rehearsal studio. She seemed like a really nice lady. When I arrived, she asked me what I wanted, and I told her that I wanted to take singing lessons. She asked me if I knew how to sing, and I told her that I did not. That was why I was there. I asked her how much the lessons would be, and she said two dollars an hour.

I agreed to take singing lessons from Leola Carter three days a week for two dollars an hour. My singing career was born in Manhattan on that day.

I had to take the train to get from Brooklyn to Manhattan. My friends told me that I was crazy. Nonetheless, on every Monday, Wednesday, and Friday, I was determined to go into the city and take my singing lessons.

I made sure that I had my own money to do this. I did not want to ask my parents for money for singing lessons (and later for acting lessons). It is amazing to me how some things just start to fall into place on their own, and end up impacting our future."

Four weeks later, Johnny began to wonder where he was going with the singing lessons. Leola assured him he was doing quite well. She pointed out to him that he could sing on key. He was getting bored, however, with just practicing notes from the musical scale. He asked if he could start singing songs.

Leola responded that her young student first needed to cultivate his voice, and that she was going to make him sound better, sing better, and understand what music was all about.

"Shortly after that, Leola told me that she was moving to 53rd and Broadway, where they had the Ed Sullivan Show. She told me that up on the tenth floor, there was a rehearsal studio. I continued to take lessons from her in the new studio."

Apparently, Leola Carter was a well-known vocal instructor. One of her students at the time was Robert Goulet. However, it was an acting coach at the studio named Robert Montague, who attracted Johnny's attention next.

"I went to him and told him that I would like to take some acting lessons. I had heard that his whole family consisted of Broadway actors, and I was told that they were pretty popular.

I started taking acting lessons from Robert Montague. Of course I continued with Leona's singing lessons as well."

In the performing world, a lucky break is sometimes all it takes to start opening doors. When someone suggested that Johnny start training as an actor and taking lessons from John Cassavetes, it turned out to be a good piece of advice – and Johnny's first lucky break.

"A friend of mine, Art Metrano -- who later worked in the *Police Academy* films -- told me, 'If acting is what you want to do, you need to go to that school.'

So I went over to the John Cassavetes school. The person in charge asked me, 'Do you know what improvisation is?'

I told him, 'I have no idea.'

He then told me that 'improv' simply meant going up on stage and making up something as you go along. He told me that he would put me up on stage with somebody, and for me to just have a conversation. Talk to my fellow actor about anything.

So I went on stage and had a conversation with another acting student. I said things like, "Hey, where do you come from? I'm not from this neighborhood.'

Suddenly, John Cassavetes walked in. He was a very popular actor at that time. He worked with Hollywood stars like Peter Falk, Anthony Franciosa, and Ben Gazzara.

I came off the stage, and he asked me what I was doing there. I told him that I wanted to be an actor, and I was taking acting lessons.

John Cassavetes then told me, 'Get outta here; go home.'

In shock, I said, 'What?'

'Go home. You can't be an actor. You're not gonna be an actor, so get out of here!'

I was a teenager at this time, and my dream – my wish beyond the stars – was going down in flames, as I trembled in front of the great John Cassavetes.

Then, he changed his tone.

'But if you really want to be an actor, don't go home.'

Later, I learned that Cassavetes did that to everybody. I was told not to pay any attention, and just continue taking acting lessons with the other twenty people in the class.

I went home, and I came back."

***

Acting lessons from John Cassavetes didn't come cheap. Students could get a discount if they paid by the month, however.

74

Johnny was working odd jobs at the time, and realized that he needed a more regular source of income -- especially if he were going to be able to continue to pay for his monthly singing and acting lessons.

"I asked my father if I could get a job with a ravioli company he had connections with, to see if I could make more money.

That was a crazy thing to ask. The workers at the ravioli company worked 12 hours a day. The company was growing so fast and selling to supermarkets all over the city. They needed double shifts to cover a full twenty-four hours of production time each day.

My father got me in, but it wasn't long before I started hating the job. At first, they had me opening and closing ravioli boxes on the assembly line. Open the box. Ravioli pours in. Close the box.

I was working this job for twelve hours a day, and feeling exhausted all the time. I tried to figure out when I could take my singing and acting lessons. It was driving me nuts. However, I was starting to make some money.

14

A MILLION MANICOTTIS

One day, the supervisor asked me if I would like to make the manicotti rather than opening and closing ravioli boxes. I told him I was interested.

The supervisor then told me that they had a store where a guy made the manicotti not far from where I lived. At that time we had moved from Kings Highway to Bay and 49th Street.

Down the street from where we were living, there it was -- a store where they made the manicotti shells and crepes. The guy was doing this work by himself and they needed another person to also make manicotti.

The store had a set-up with six burners, six frying pans, and a bucket of liquid dough. The guy taught me how to use a scoop to make the manicotti.

I soon became the 'manicotti guy.' Working twelve hours a day, from six at night until six in the morning, I must have easily rolled out a million manicottis. I wasn't just the 'manicotti guy.'

I was King Manicotti!"

***

Meanwhile, Johnny continued to keep up with his singing and acting lessons. After creating a million manicottis, he knew in his heart of hearts that his dream was leading him in a much different direction.

"One day, I was in New York for my lessons. I noticed a bum standing outside the studio. His name was Johnny Baron, and he was an honest-to-God street bum. At night, he would slip into the building, hide in the basement, and sleep near the boiler.

As I was entering the building one day, Johnny Baron asked me what I was doing. I said that I was taking singing lessons. He told me that he wrote songs and would let me hear some of the songs that he wrote. By this time I was 18 years old.

Johnny Baron told me that he had a song called *Babysitting Baby*. The timing was perfect. Elvis was famous, and so was Bobby Darin. Frankie Avalon was also on the rise in popularity.

Johnny Baron told me that I needed to hear his song. I told him that I was walking up Broadway to get a bite to eat at The Turf, where a lot of wannabe singers hung out.

They had the best cheesecake in the whole world, and an unbelievable hamburger. The Turf was on 49th Street and Broadway, right past Jack Dempsey's place.

I told Johnny Baron to come with me to The Turf. I bought him a cup of coffee and a hamburger because he had no money. He told me that he could not sing the song to me at The Turf because they stole songs there.

He was right. Years ago, if you were not in a private place, people would pick up the melody and -- before you knew it -- your song belonged to somebody else."

15

BABYSITTING BABY

Johnny Martino sensed that he was on to something with a lot of potential. Baron and Johnny did get together in a secure environment, and Baron eventually sang *Babysitting Baby* to Johnny.

"Johnny Baron had also written another song called *Having A Race With Time*. I quickly learned both songs, and asked him who we could get to arrange them.

He recommended a guy named Samson Horton. Baron didn't know him very well, but he knew that Samson hung around The Turf. Samson had two hit songs out at the time – *La-Di-Da*, and a huge chartbuster called *Silhouette*.

We met with Samson and he told me how much it would cost to do the two songs.

I had been rehearsing them over and over. I went home, and I was really excited. In my mind, I kept thinking: Johnny Martino is on his way to recording his first two songs.

I told my father that I needed $500 to record the songs, and mentioned that I had a couple hundred dollars saved up.

My father looked at me and said, 'That's a lot of money. What are you -- crazy? Forget about it.'

After he thought about it for awhile, my father brought the subject back up. He asked me if I really wanted to sing. I assured him that I did. He asked, 'What are you a Frank Sinatra? You ain't gonna be Frank Sinatra!'

I looked my father straight in the eye and said, 'Pa, I'm not Frank Sinatra, but I am going to give it a try. I've been taking voice lessons, studying hard, and I want to do it.'

My brother Jackie, who died of lung cancer at only 48 years old, went to bat for me on this. He told my father that he would put up some of the money, and my father could put in some also.

'We will all chip in. The kid's been taking lessons,' said Jackie.

My father asked who was going to do the music. I told him I had a guy who was an arranger, and he had some hit music on the radio.

Between the three of us, we came up with the $500, and my brother Jackie and I drove into Manhattan.

When Jackie saw that Samson was a black guy, he became a little hesitant. Remember, this was before the Civil Rights era.

I told Jackie that Samson was an arranger, and reminded him that there were a lot of successful black musicians, especially performers like Nat King Cole.

Jackie started to relax, and we all sat around a table at The Turf and had lunch. Samson told us that for $500 he would *guarantee* that the record would be cut. He would bring in the musicians and write the arrangements.

Then he told my brother that I had been rehearsing, and that I was really good.

The next thing I knew, I recorded the song *Babysitting Baby*."

***

In the pre-Beatles Rock and Roll era, teenagers spent hours talking to each other on the telephone. Their love affair with the phone probably took second place only to their love affairs with each other.

Who can forget the opening telephone sequence in the Broadway musical *Bye Bye Birdie*? Those who grew up during that time will forever remember the Big Bopper's phone call in *Chantilly Lace*.

The Big Bopper only had one hit song before dying in a plane crash with Buddy Holly and Richie Valens. Yet his song has become immortal.

The record starts with the phone ringing. The Big Bopper answers, in that distinctive rich bass voice of his. We hear his side of the conversation with his heart-throb listening in on the other end of the phone.

Then the song actually begins. "Chantilly lace and a pony-tail hanging down....Oh, Baby, That's what I like!"

Babysitting Baby had a similar opening. As the record begins, the phone rings. Johnny Martino, in a sexy voice, says, "Hello."

The girl replies, "I'm lonesome. Just thought I'd call."

The music then fires up, with "Whatcha doing baby, babysitting baby?"

Johnny recalls that, "it was such a cute tune. I was very excited after recording it. The flip side was Johnny Baron's beautiful ballad -- *Having a Race With Time*."

Johnny had so much faith in his first record, that he took it all the way to the top – Capitol Records.

"I couldn't believe it. Capitol Records didn't want it. So I took my demo around to this label and that label, but everybody threw me out.

So now I started wondering, 'How I am going to sell my record?' More importantly, I started wondering how I was going to tell my father that we had lost the $500 investment. I did not give up though. The name of this game is that you don't ever give up."

Johnny then took the record to a company called Tin Pan Alley, located in the Brill Building at 49th Street and Broadway – in fact, right above The Turf.

The newly minted recording artist wasted no time knocking on doors. Finally, he came to an office of a record label representative who must have seen better times. The man had no
84

desk and was seated on an old orange crate. An ancient portable Victrola sat on a nearby stand.

"The guy answered the door and asked me what I wanted. I told him that I had a record, and asked if he had a record company label. He said that he was *with* a label.

I gave him the record and he played it on that old RCA Victrola. He listened, said that it was cute, and asked me what I wanted to do with it.

I told him that I wanted to get it on a label, and have it aired on the radio. He asked me if I could leave that copy with him and I told him sure. I gave him my phone number and left.

A few days later he called me and told me that he was going to sign me up and give me a contract with three percent of the record sales.

I said, 'No money up front?

The agent replied, 'No, kid. You're just starting out. When we get this thing on the radio, your name will be out there.'

He wasn't kidding. A few days later, he called me up and told me that on Friday night, WABC was going to play my record. I tried hard to keep the excitement out of my voice.

'WABC with Scott Muni?"

'Yeah, Scott Muni, Dan Ingram, Cousin Brucie, and all the other personalities. They are all going to be playing your record on WABC.'

I couldn't wait to tell my family."

Friday evening arrived.

The entire Martino family gathered around the radio in the dining room. The unmistakable voice of Dean Martin came over the airwaves. Dean's song finished up, and the DJ followed it with......"Johnny Martino singing *Babysitting Baby*!"

Nobody in the room moved. Everyone seemed to have the same thought: "Oh my gosh! Johnny's record is playing on the radio."

"The next thing I know, the song was playing two or three times a day. Then I started getting requests to do record hops. My record guy would call me up and tell me that I was going to Long Island, going here, and going there.

He told me that I would be singing the song at record hops with all of the other singers who had records coming out.

'This is how you promote the song,' he told me.

Before long, it seemed like I was singing the song everywhere. After a performance, as I exited the stage, the teenaged girls would all flock around and reach out to touch my hair or clothes.

One day was particularly chaotic, and the super-charged girls ended up tearing my silk shirt before I could get safely away.

When I arrived home, the shirt was so torn up that my mother thought I had been in a street fight.

During the *Babysitting Baby* days, I was really doing well -- and loving every minute of seeing my wish upon the stars coming true. I was becoming a teen idol. The kids were all screaming out in the audience, and I have to admit that I was cute back then."

***

With *Babysitting Baby* playing regularly on the radio, and Johnny performing at record hops throughout New York City, it appeared that his musical career was about to take off nationally. If only he could break into television.

In August, the first TV break materialized, and Johnny appeared on a local show that had seemingly aired forever -- *Joe Franklin's Memory Lane.*

"I went on the show, and after that, the response was so good that my record agent called me up and told me the really big news: I was going to perform on the *Dick Clark Show* on August 13, 1958, in Philadelphia.

What could I say? It was an offer I couldn't refuse!

I told my father that I had to get to Philadelphia, and asked him if he knew how to get there. He told me that he knew how to get there.

Now *he* was extremely excited. Not only could he listen to me on the radio, but everyone he knew was talking about his son Johnny Martino's *Babysitting Baby.*

I remember getting into the car that day. Pop had a beautiful Cadillac. We drove to Philadelphia with my brother Pete coming along for the ride.

I know that the Dick Clark show was very popular at the time. The TV Guide that week featured Steve Lawrence and Edie Gorme on the cover. I am listed in that TV Guide as a guest star on *The Dick Clark Show* (which he later named *American Bandstand).*

After arriving in Philadelphia, my father had no problem finding the local ABC affiliate. The TV station was housed in a very large studio.

The first thing we noticed was the long line outside the building. At that point, I start to get a little nervous. I'm thinking, 'Oh my God! *The Dick Clark Show*!

I knew that the show would be telecast in front of a live audience. There would be no recording and no editing. In other words, there would be no room for mistakes. My performance had to be perfect.

I couldn't have been in the studio more than a couple minutes, when a production assistant spotted me.

'John Martino. Come on over here. Quick!'

A couple of other production assistants hustled me into a dressing room and told me to change out of my street clothes and into my TV outfit.

I finally made it to a holding area, where performers waited prior to going on-stage.

There I met a group called The Aqua-tones. They also had a record out at that time. I learned later that they were extremely disappointed to see me. It seems that the producers would bring in substitute entertainment, just in case the head-liner did not show up.

The Aqua-tones were more than disappointed to be shaking hands with me. Johnny Martino was the last person they wanted to see in that studio that day.

It was 3:15 in the afternoon. A producer came up to me and said, 'Come on, John. You're gonna be in front of a crane, and there is going to be a phone on the top of the stand.'

I asked him what the phone was for, and he said, 'You're gonna answer the phone. That's your record right?'

I said, 'Okay.' How do I know what I am supposed to do with this phone?

I asked the guy how many people would be watching, and he told me, 'I don't know, maybe thirty million.'

I said, 'WHAT?'

He told me that it was the hottest TV show on television. I asked again if I were doing this thing live, and he told me, 'Yeah. You can't make a mistake.'

Showtime!

There I am, standing in front of this crane, ready to go on. I hear a voice announce *Johnny Martino*. The phone rings, I pick it up.

Thirty million viewers hear a girl say, 'Hello. I'm lonesome, Baby. Just thought I'd call and find out whatcha doing, Baby.'

I put the phone down, and my adrenaline was pumping. Studio dancers were performing behind me, as I belted out my song. When I finished, the studio audience erupted into a deafening roar. All of the girls were screaming. At that moment, I felt like a super-star.

Off-stage, a production assistant ushered me to an autograph table. When the show ended, the teenagers in the audience rushed over.

I had brought a hundred publicity photos with me, but they were all gone in a matter of minutes. After that, I was autographing scraps of paper, hands, and whatever else the kids had with them that could be autographed. It seemed like an endless flow of fans were coming up to the table to see me, talk to me, and get my autograph.

My father and brother were standing on the side, watching. They could not believe it. They had to be wondering, 'What is he doing, signing all of those autographs? How famous is he becoming?' It was amazing."

***

Around this time in his life, Johnny's brothers all seemed to be walking down the aisle and starting their own families.

"I met a girl too. I was 21 at the time, and I still had the teenagers screaming for me, pulling at my shirt, and always flirting. It just wasn't the type of atmosphere conducive to marriage.

We were blessed and had a beautiful little girl. That first segment of my married life was destined to be a brief one. My second marriage lasted twenty-three years, and produced three more adorable daughters. However, that marriage also became a casualty of my career."

16

OFF TO HOLLYWOOD

In 1960, despite one hit song, Johnny's career as a singer was going nowhere. He started thinking about heading to the West Coast and pursuing his dream in acting.

"I told my family that I was going to California. They thought I was crazy. How could I go to California? I had no money. I just told them that I was going.

I looked in the newspaper ads for a car to get me to California. I didn't have any money to buy one, but -- back in those days -- you could sometimes find someone who wanted a car delivered somewhere.

Once again, my lucky stars came into play. There in the classified section of the newspaper was someone in New York who had a 1958 Ford convertible. He wanted it delivered to the Hollywood Roosevelt Hotel on Hollywood Boulevard in ten days. The driver would have to pay for the gas.

I contacted the person and agreed to deliver the car. I picked up the convertible, had a $100 in my pocket, and headed out cross-country for California.

I remember arriving in Hollywood and riding down Sunset Boulevard, thinking, 'My God. I'm in Hollywood, California. Can you believe it?'

It was like a dream come true.

I knew that I had to get a job. Most of my hundred bucks was gone by the time I arrived. I wondered what I was going to do. I had no money but I sure was not going to write home for any. I never wanted to ask for money from home. I said to myself, 'Johnny needs to do this on his own.'

As I was driving around, I spotted a guy on the corner, yelling, 'Get your map to the movie stars' homes. Get your map.'

I pulled over to the curb and opened the window. I asked him how much. I think that he said they were a dollar. So I invested a dollar for a map of the movie stars' homes."

One thing about Johnny Martino -- he has never turned down an opportunity to do something unusual. Even better, if that unusual something also happened to be filled with fun and adventure.

So, rather than do something practical and look for a place to live in Los Angeles, Johnny decided it would be more exciting to visit a movie star at home. What better celebrity than his singing idol and fellow Italian, Frank Sinatra?

"I drove into Beverly Hills, and with the help of my star map, I located Frank's street. I passed by one huge mansion after another.

94

I had just arrived in town, and I did not go anywhere other than Beverly Hills where Frank Sinatra lived. It was crazy.

I pulled up in front of Frank Sinatra's house, got out of the car, and went up to the porch to ring the door-bell.

A lady answered the door. 'Can I help you?'

'I'd like to speak to Mr. Sinatra.'

The lady told me that Frank no longer lived there, and that he had sold her the house two years ago. I asked her if she knew where he lived now, and she said that she did. She told me that he lived at the top of Coldwater Canyon."

Within minutes, Johnny had established a good rapport with the woman. She stepped out of the house, and pointed toward a large antenna on top of a mountain, which was visible from her house. She explained that Sinatra landed his helicopter there. The antenna marked the spot where his house was located.

Johnny asked for directions, and the lady directed him back down Sunset Boulevard to Coldwater Canyon. Noticing his Brooklyn accent, she asked if Johnny had ever driven in the mountains before.

When he told her no, the woman explained that the road up the mountain was winding and dangerous, so he would need to be careful. She then wished him good luck, and he headed out to visit Frank Sinatra.

"I was driving up the mountain, round and round, with lots of turns. At the same time, I was trying to figure out where the house was located.

I finally arrived at the top of the mountain and spotted the antenna. The house was a big Oriental-style home, with huge columns and a gigantic gate in front.

I began wondering what to do next. Getting there was the easy part. Now what?

On the side of the porch columns, I spotted a door-bell. I got out of the car and went up to the door. A small sign was posted by the doorbell: 'If you ring this bell, you better have a damn good reason.'

What, is he kidding me with this doorbell? I'm Johnny Martino from Brooklyn. It didn't dawn on me at the time that maybe the great Frank Sinatra didn't even watch *The Dick Clark Show*.

I swear that I heard his voice

'Hey, who is it?

'Hey Frank. It's Johnny Martino.'

I laugh about this now, but I was a nut job back then. Within moments, a security guard came out to the gate.

'Hey kid, whadda you want?'

'Whadda I want? I want to talk to Frankie.'

The guard asks me, 'Do you have an appointment?'

'No.'

'You have to have an appointment. You can't just come up here, and ring the bell, and talk to Frank Sinatra. Call his agent.'

I told the guard that I would get in touch with Frank through his agent and thanked him for his time. I then left.

About this time, I realized that I didn't have any place to stay. My biggest accomplishment after arriving in Los Angeles was ringing Frank Sinatra's doorbell. What next?

I drove back down the hill and headed out on Santa Monica Boulevard. Before long, I came across a gigantic cathedral with gorgeous statues.

Across the street from the cathedral was a tiny place called the Deseret Motel. It looked like the kind of place that would fit my budget.

I went in and asked the desk clerk about the room rates. Six dollars a night sounded perfect, so my first temporary residence in Los Angeles would be the Deseret Motel. I sure wouldn't have to go very far to go to church!

Once I settled in, I couldn't resist looking at my *Homes of the Stars* map again.

One of my favorite actors at the time was an Italian guy named Tony Franciosa. A lot of people ask, 'Who was Tony Franciosa?' Actually, he was very famous back then.

Tony Franciosa starred in a movie called *Wild is the Wind* with Anthony Quinn. He did several other major movies, including *The Long, Hot Summer*, and *A Face in the Crowd*, as

97

well as television shows such as *The Twilight Zone, Naked City*, and *The Love Boat*. Tony was a great actor. He was one of my favorites because I felt I resembled him.

The *Homes of the Stars* map led me to a place labeled Tony Franciosa's home. I got out of the car, went up to the house, and knocked on the door.

Tony Franciosa was not the person who came to the door. To my amazement, it was Shelley Winters.

I quickly recovered my composure.

'Is Tony Franciosa here?'

'No, he's not here.'

She was definitely not in a good mood. I asked her if she knew where I could find him, but she told me that she was sorry, but she could not tell me.

Shelley Winters then closed the door.

As I was walking down the walkway back to the car, the door opened again, and a black woman who appeared to be the maid beckoned to me.

'Young man.' she whispered, 'He lives in the Chateau Marmont on Sunset Boulevard.'

Chateau Marmont? I never heard of it. I asked her where that was, and she gave me some general directions and told me that I couldn't miss it. It was a very big hotel. I thanked her for the information and headed off for the Chateau Marmont.

Tony Franciosa's former maid was a great source of information. I also found out from her that Tony and Shelley

98

Winters had just broken up. No wonder why Miss Winters seemed so angry and unfriendly.

I arrived at the Chateau Marmont without any problems, and pulled into the driveway. That's where I almost literally went into shock.

Standing out front waiting for his car was Frankenstein! That's right. Frankenstein! I recognized the one and only Boris Karloff immediately.

I quickly parked the car, but by the time I arrived out front, Karloff was gone. Who should I bump into instead? An actress named Patricia Medina and Joseph Cotton.

By this time, you must realize that I was a lot of things, but shy was not one of them. I introduced myself to Cotton, who was cordial and replied, 'Nice to meet you, Mr. Martino.'

If ever I had any doubts about where I was, those doubts were gone. I was in Hollywood!

Before all of this star-gazing took place, I asked the parking attendant if Anthony Franciosa was there. Tony's real name was Anthony Franciosa.

The parking attendant told me that he had been there a minute ago, and that he was in and out all day. I asked him if he would mind if I left the car there for a few minutes because I wanted to grab a burger. He told me, 'Sure.'

As I was leaving, I said to him, Tell Tony Franciosa that Johnny Martino was here.'

I left the parking lot by the hotel and I went to get a bite to eat. When I came back, I spotted the same parking attendant.

'By the way, did Tony Franciosa come back?'

'Yeah, he's upstairs.'

I asked him if he would mind if I went through the garage instead of the lobby. He told me to go ahead, and mentioned that there was an elevator. I asked him what room Tony was in. I think I remember him saying 7-F. It was on the 5th floor.

Of course, I was a little bit nervous going up to see Tony Franciosa. I found the room with no problem, and I pressed the doorbell.

The easily recognizable Tony Franciosa opened the door and said, 'Johnny Martino.' He had a great smile on his face.

I said, 'That's me.'

Franciosa then invited me in and asked, 'What can I do for you?'

'Tony, I just drove in from New York. I don't know if there is anything that you can do, but I'll tell you why I'm here.'

I then launched into my story, while a big name movie star listened attentively to every word. I felt I had really arrived in Hollywood."

Johnny had an all-encompassing conversation with Tony Franciosa that day. He went into detail about his acting and singing lessons, his *Babysitting Baby* record, and his television appearance with Dick Clark.

"I told him that I came to town and I wanted to find a little job so that I could support myself, and try to get into the business. He asked me where I was staying and I mentioned the Deseret Motel.

'Alright, how about I give you a call later today? You'll do anything?'

'Whatever you can get for me I will take -- any kind of job.'

We shook hands, and I headed out of the apartment and back to my car. I was on Cloud Nine. I now had none other than Tony Franciosa looking for some work for me -- work which would pay my bills while I was trying to make my wish come true by jump-starting an acting career in Hollywood.

Late that same night back at the motel, the phone rang. I picked up the receiver.

'Hello. It's Tony Franciosa. There's a restaurant in Beverly Hills on Little Santa Monica Boulevard. Are you far from there?'

I told him that I was really not that far away, and that I would find it. Franciosa told me to go to the restaurant the next night at about 4 o'clock, wearing a white shirt and black slacks. He told me that I was going to bus tables.

I told Tony that would be great. He assured me that it was a very nice restaurant and that I would like it. I thanked Tony for helping me. He told me that someday he would come by the restaurant and see me. I thanked him again and hung up.

17

LA SCALA

The next day I put on black slacks and had to go get a white shirt. Believe it or not, I did not have a white shirt.

I reported to the restaurant -- La Scala -- and asked for the maitre'd. He was a guy from New Jersey named Mateo. I recognized his accent right away. He was a well-dressed guy, really sharp.

When I introduced myself, Mateo said, 'Anthony Franciosa told me that you were coming. You ever bus tables before?'

I told Mateo no. He called out to a guy named Jose. Jose came from the back room, and Mateo told him to show me how to set the tables, along with everything else that I had to do.

Jose said to me, 'John, we get a lot of famous people here, so just treat them like regular people -- because they are just people.' I told him alright.

Jose was a really nice guy. In no time, he taught me how to set up the tables with the napkins, glasses, and silverware.

Around 6:30 PM on my first night at La Scala, I was walking around re-setting the tables of the customers who had finished eating.

La Scala had a bar in front, facing the main street. There was also a back entrance off of the kitchen. I noticed people started coming in from the back, through the kitchen, and into a little alcove where I had to pick up the Italian bread for the tables.

The next thing I knew, there was Betty Grable, Richard Conte and a very beautiful young lady I didn't recognize. They had come in the back way and were talking about the Gerber Baby on the baby-food jars.

I couldn't help over-hearing the conversation. Betty chimed in, saying that she was a Gerber Baby. The girls were talking and smiling, and Richard Conte was taking it all in. Richard Conte! He was one of my idols. Little did either of us know that twelve years later, he and I would both be working in a movie together called *The Godfather*.

That first night at La Scala was a real-eye-opener for me. I recognized Fernando Lamas and Esther Williams at the table right next to Conte and Grable. Across from them sat Natalie Wood and Robert Wagner. Apparently, they had all come in the back entrance.

It was difficult trying to remember all of the protocol connected with setting up the tables. I was much too distracted. I could not believe that all of these famous people were right in the same room with me."

Celebrities continued to pour into La Scala from the back entrance. In the last booth right near the kitchen, Johnny spotted Rod Taylor dining with a beautiful Asian girl.

Rod Taylor, as you may recall, was featured in the movie, *The Birds*.

As Jose demonstrated the proper way to carry a tray after cleaning off a table, Johnny discovered that he was more than fascinated by the famous clientele dining in La Scala that night. He was downright nervous. Who in their right mind would want to make a fool of themselves in front of that glamorous group?

Johnny began to concentrate on the proper way to carry a tray without dropping it. He started fantasizing about the horrible consequences of dropping one of those trays. Little did he know, that he was working his mental state up to a point where he could become a victim of his own self-fulfilling prophecy.

As Johnny moved from the restaurant to the kitchen, with a loaded tray held at head level, only one thought went through his mind: "Don't drop the tray. Don't drop the tray."

Johnny was concentrating so hard on his tray-carrying technique, that he failed to see he was going into the kitchen through the door marked OUT.

At the same time, another employee was heading into the restaurant in the opposite direction through the same door.

BOOM!!!

Suddenly, all eyes in the restaurant were on Johnny Martino in his unexpected and unwanted opening night performance at La Scala.

"The tray went up in the air towards me. I was trying desperately to balance the tray, but it was no use. Things were going all over the floor.

The place was full of movie stars staring at a bus-boy helplessly watching the entire contents of his tray cascading to the floor.

Mortified, I stooped down and started picking up the mess. I could hear conversations start to resume again. I can only imagine what everyone was talking about. My worst fears were realized. I dropped a tray!"

Johnny continued to pick up tray items from the floor and return them to the kitchen. When he re-entered the dining room, the embarrassed bus-boy saw Rod Taylor looking in his direction. Taylor beckoned to him.

"You know, down the street is 20th Century Fox. I'm doing a show there called *Hong Kong.* When you get a chance, drop by the studio and tell them that I told you to come in."

Johnny assured Rod Taylor that he would come by 20th Century Fox at his earliest convenience. Recognizing a moment of opportunity, Johnny shared his background with Taylor. Maybe the night hadn't been such a disaster after all.

"I did follow up on Rod Taylor's invitation. I went over to 20th Century Fox Studios during the day. I got to the gate and told the guard, 'My name is Johnny Martino, and Rod Taylor told me to come and see him.'

106

The guard looked at a list of names and said, 'Ain't no-one named Johnny Martino here.'

I was kind of shocked, but asked the guard if Rod Taylor was on the lot that day. He told me that he was.

I started walking away, thinking I had to get in the gates somehow. The guard-booth window was about five feet high off of the ground. I returned to the guard-shack, bent over low so that I would pass underneath the window, and entered the 20th Century Fox Studio. No one had seen me make my first entrance into a movie studio -- hunched over and running!"

Johnny's first impressions of a movie studio are as fresh today as they were more than fifty years ago. He can still visualize in great detail the various sets and false fronts spread all across the 20th Century Fox lot.

Walking around in total amazement and wonder, Johnny eventually stumbled onto the *Hong Kong* set where Rod Taylor was filming. Everyone assumed the handsome young man dressed in a nice leather jacket belonged on the set.

As he stood quietly watching scenes being filmed, Johnny was convinced beyond a doubt that acting would be his life-long career.

"When Rod Taylor finished shooting his last scene, I called to him. 'Mr. Taylor!'

He turned around, saw me, and came walking over. I reminded him that I was the busboy with the flying tray.

107

'Johnny Martino. Let me introduce you to someone special. She's pretty famous.' He beckoned to an attractive woman on the set who joined us. She turned out to be Ida Lupino.

'Ida. I want you to meet Johnny Martino. He's a singer from New York and was on Dick Clark's show.'

'Johnny, nice to meet you. My pleasure.'

That night, I reflected back on my brief career as a bus-boy at La Scala. I was paying the motel six dollars per day. I was making tips at night, because it was the custom for the waiters to give a small percentage to the bus-boys.

The year was 1960, and I was bringing home between twelve and fifteen dollars a night. That was nice money back then. I was able to put money up and build some savings.

The first couple of nights I had to take a bus. It was 11 o'clock at night, and I was taking a bus home in the heart of a major metropolitan area.

Back then, hitchhiking was a whole lot safer. So occasionally, while I was waiting for the bus, drivers would stop and ask me if I wanted a ride. I would decline the ride and just wait for the bus.

One night I wrote a song which I called, *Oh Lord Up Above*. I was sitting on the bench at my bus-stop, looking at the stars. There I was -- sitting in Beverly Hills, looking at the stars, making a wish, and writing a song."

The next day, Johnny headed back to work at La Scala, a mere forty-eight hours after dropping his tray in front of a roomful of celebrities.

He remembers working in a little alcove slicing a large basket of bread. As a glamorous-looking customer tried to squeeze through the alcove, Johnny bumped her with his left elbow while trying to slice the bread. He turned around to apologize, but couldn't find the right words.

"I was face-to-face with Marilyn Monroe. We were no more than six inches apart in that tiny space. She was a little bit shorter than me. I was trying to gather my thoughts, thinking to myself, 'My God! It's Marilyn Monroe.'

I finally get a few words of apology out, and she smiled and said, 'It's okay.'

Marilyn Monroe was very sweet. She then walked by me and went to a corner table along the back wall. I had the impression that it was almost like her private table. She sat in the booth all by herself. There were two-seater tables right across from her, but she sat quiet and alone in a booth for four.

Later on that night, someone came in and tapped me on the shoulder. When I turned around and saw who it was, I had another one of those heart-stopping moments. It was Fred Astaire.

'Mr. Astaire, how ya doing?

'Alright kid, what's going on? How about a table for four?'

I told him no problem. I ran to the maître'd and told him that Fred Astaire needed a table for four. He told me, 'John, the place is packed. Tell him to go sit at the bar.'

I was shocked. Go tell Fred Astaire to sit at the bar until a table was ready?

So in fancy Beverly Hills restaurants-- just like ordinary people have to do in restaurants that are packed -- you wait for a table, no matter who you are!

I went back to Fred Astaire and I was a little embarrassed.

'Mr. Astaire, would you mind sitting at the bar until we get a table?'

Fred Astaire was a very classy guy.

'No, that's alright. Maybe we'll stop and have a drink before we eat.'

18

SINATRA'S VILLA CAPRI

"I was meeting a lot of famous people -- Rod Taylor, Ida Lupino, Marilyn Monroe, Fred Astaire. I started to wonder how I could get to where they were in life.

When I was on the *Hong Kong* set with Rod Taylor, he told me to go see Robert Walker, the casting director. Taylor even arranged for a car to take me to the casting office."

Johnny's arrival at Robert Walker's casting office represented the first time he ever interviewed for work in

Hollywood as an actor. In his interview, Johnny described his studies with John Cassavetes, and also mentioned his singing career.

Johnny admitted that his acting credits were on the light side, but he was looking for that first big break that could earn him his Screen Actors Guild card. SAG membership is essential for anyone hoping to appear in the movies as more than an extra.

At the conclusion of the interview, Walker told the aspiring young actor from New York City to get some head-shots made, and bring them back to him. He would see what he could do to help Johnny out.

Head-shots are considered a vital tool for every actor. They are 8x10 photographs of a performer's head and shoulders, and are used extensively by agents and casting directors to determine if an actor has 'the right look' for a part in a movie or television show.

Although Walker never came through with an acting job, he did steer the bus-boy who elbowed Marilyn Monroe in the right direction. With head-shots in hand, Johnny was ready to tackle other casting directors in Hollywood.

"I called my father and said, 'Pa, here's how I'm making out.' I told him everything that I was doing. He mentioned that he had a friend who lived in Hollywood who was originally from Brooklyn. Pop told me that he would give me the guy's phone number, and I was to call him. Pop knew that I did not have a car anymore, so he said the guy would pick me up.

I called the guy on the phone. His name was Jimmy. I introduced myself and he asked me how I was doing. Then he asked me where I was, and I told him that I was at the Deseret Motel.

A short while later, Jimmy came by the motel and took me to his house in Hollywood. Jimmy lived in a very nice colonial home. When we arrived, his wife Nancy had dinner just about ready. I joined the family for the first home-cooked meal I had eaten in quite a while.

After dinner, Jimmy told me that we were going to take a ride to a restaurant nearby in Hollywood. There was someone there he wanted me to meet.

We drove down the road from where he lived to a street called Yucca, pulling up in front of a restaurant called the Villa Capri.

It turned out that Patsy D'Amore and Frank Sinatra owned the restaurant. We went in and Jimmy introduced me to Patsy. I could tell that they all knew Jimmy and respected him. There were other guys originally from New York hanging out at this place also.

Patsy asked me if I wanted to work there. In fact, he told me that I absolutely could come and work there.

I thought that would be nice, but said that I had to give notice to the La Scala. Patsy told me that would be fine. Just

115

come by whenever I was ready. I had the job whenever I wanted it.

It looked like I was at least moving up in the Los Angeles restaurant business. Even though La Scala had a celebrity clientele that was second to none, the Villa Capri was a larger, much more elegant restaurant.

Back at Jimmy's house, he told me that down the road from him were some apartments that could be rented for $40 a month. That sure beat the Deseret Motel at six dollars a day.

Jimmy described the place as having small one-room furnished apartments. He told me that I should live there, not only to save money. It just so happened that the Villa Capri was close by also.

Soon after, I left La Scala and moved out of the motel. I had a few dollars saved up from the few weeks that I was there, and I moved into the little apartment near the Villa Capri.

Back in those days, Los Angeles was not as congested as it is today. There was less smog, and apartment complexes like mine frequently advertised one month of free rent.

The first thing I noticed when I went to work at the Villa Capri was their clientele – much different from La Scala.

The celebrities dining at Villa Capri were a couple notches down from super-star status. Nevertheless, the restaurant did attract its share of big names.

Glenn Ford ate there, and so did Elizabeth Taylor. Even Sir Lawrence Olivier came in one time.

One night, Frank Sinatra dropped by, but he came in a little bit late. Usually at around 10 o'clock, the tables and chairs were broken down, and we were told to start closing up the place.

Frankie came in with about four or five people. He called out, 'Let's get going. Let's have a little party here.'

I was thrilled because here in the same room with me was Frank Sinatra. Prior to then, I had only been as close to him as his doorbell.

The one and only -- Frank Sinatra -- came in and sat down. The staff quickly prepared a table for Frank's group. They stayed for quite a while. I did not say anything to him. It was enough for me just to be in the same room with my idol. There he was. Frank Sinatra -- live and in person.

Back in the 1940's, I first saw Frankie at the Paramount with my brother Petey. I said something crazy that night. I don't know why. I was a little kid around seven or eight years old.

I asked Pete, 'Is that Frank Sinatra the real skin?'

I don't know why I said 'the real skin.' Maybe I was thinking he could have been a puppet or robot or something.

My brother told me that it was the real Frank Sinatra standing on the stage. We were up in the balcony. He was a teenager at the time. He took me to see Frankie because he knew that I loved Sinatra.

Now here I was in my idol's presence once again. The guy sitting in the restaurant was definitely 'the real skin.'

I wanted to go over and say something to him, but I just didn't do it. I think maybe I got a little nervous after going to his house and ringing the doorbell.

***

Working at the Villa Capri allowed me to save good tips. I learned how to do the cappuccino bar. They taught me how to make the best cappuccino in the world. My mentor was from northern Italy, and his recipe was amazing.

One Sunday night in 1960, right before the election, I was at the cappuccino bar, and in walked Democratic presidential candidate John F. Kennedy with three other men.

119

Kennedy was seated at Table #1, and after dinner he ordered a cappuccino. I made four of the Villa Capri special recipe cappuccinos, starting with fresh espresso from the machine.

I added vanilla ice cream and chocolate ice cream, as well as half and half cream. Then I melted it all down. As a final touch, I foamed each one all the way up, and added a drop of Rye and a drop of Southern Comfort to the foam. I then brought the drinks to Table #1.

While I was back at my station, the waiter came running up and said, 'That Kennedy guy wants to talk to you.'

I went back to the table and John F. Kennedy looked at me and asked, 'What do you put in the cappuccino?'

I told him that it was a private recipe and that I was not supposed to tell him. He told me that he did not want to write it down or anything; he just wanted to know what it was.

So I told the next president of the United States that I used vanilla ice cream, chocolate ice cream, half and half cream, espresso and a drop of Southern Comfort and Rye.

He then asked me if I put actual liquor in the drink. I told him that I did, unless a customer was under-age. I mentioned that the liquor gave the drink a little bit of extra flavor.

Kennedy told me that it was really amazing -- a great drink. He thanked me and shook my hand. I then blurted out, 'You know, I'm gonna vote for you.'

120

Little did my famous cappuccino customer know that he had already come in contact with my family before that night at the Villa Capri – at the Kefauver senate crime committee hearings.

Gaetano Martino testifying at the Kefauver hearing

122

19

LUCKY SHEDS A TEAR

Back in 1951, John F. Kennedy was part of the Kefauver Senate Committee investigating organized crime in America. My father was one of the people who received a notice from the government to appear before the committee. Investigators had learned about our family association with Lucky Luciano, and the senators wanted to ask questions about my dad's relationship to Lucky.

My father arrived in Washington, and answered all of the questions that the senators asked. He told them that there was no exchange with Lucky financially. We simply had a close family relationship. He even talked to Congress about my brother Charlie's confirmation in Sicily. Then he was excused and returned home.

A few days later, my father received an official letter from the government, stating that -- because of his special relationship with Lucky Luciano -- he could not go back to Italy without an escort.

In a follow-up visit, federal agents asked my father about Joe Adonis. They asked him about the three cars Dad brought to Italy, and the reason why he brought them.

My father told them that they were all friends and he brought them cars as gifts. I believe he spoke honestly and truthfully."

***

The 1950's produced another memorable moment for Johnny Martino. One day, while on the subway returning home from his acting and singing lessons, Johnny spotted a headline in the newspaper: LUCKY SHEDS A TEAR.

"I picked up the discarded newspaper and began to read the article. I wondered why Lucky would shed a tear. Then I found out.

Igea Lissoni, the girl that Lucky Luciano fell so madly in love with, had died of cancer. I couldn't believe it -- the beautiful and loving Igea, who had been so wonderful to me and my brother Charlie. She was only in her thirties when she passed away.

I was on the train and began to cry. I arrived home, not sure if my mother had heard the news or not. I told her the news in Italian. When my father heard about it, he was devastated. He knew that Igea was the love of Lucky Luciano's life.

Lucky had told Igea that – of all the women that he had been with throughout his life -- she was the one that he would marry in a heartbeat.

Lucky told Igea that he loved her so much, that he would take his heart out and give it to her. He did not think that he needed to sign a piece of paper to make it legal.

Igea understood how he felt, and knew that she was the love of his life, so she accepted just living with him and sharing in that love.

This had to be the most beautiful relationship that I have ever witnessed. I will always remember that it was with a little bit of persistence by my mother that Lucky was able to successfully pursue this young, beautiful lady.

Many years later, I found a parallel in my own love life. I am no Lucky Luciano. I am Johnny Martino, just a kid who met a man of that magnitude early in my life. I did not know what he was at that time, but after I learned more about Lucky Luciano, I realized that his public image displayed only part of the true person Lucky Luciano really was -- not to mention what he was able to do during his lifetime.

Lucky had many good personal qualities. He was someone I will always remember fondly. Only recently, has it come to light that he was working secretly with Naval Intelligence during World War II.

That contribution to his country in a time of war undoubtedly saved countless young American lives during the invasion of Sicily.

In many ways, I believe Lucky Luciano more than paid his debt to society. He was a true-blue American, and he loved -- and faithfully served -- his adopted country."

Lucky Luciano with Igea and friends

20

THE FAVOR

"I stuck it out working at the Villa Capri for awhile. One day, my father decided to come visit me in California. There were a couple of guys at the Villa Capri from Brooklyn who knew my father. They were all waiting for him in the Jimmy Durante Room, one of the restaurant's largest dining areas.

My father was ushered in to a seat at the head of the table. It was interesting, watching all of these guys from New York just sitting around the table and enjoying my dad's company.

The next day my father told me that he had to visit someone else he knew, who moved from New York to California. His name was also Giovanni, and my father showed me his address. I told him we could find this person. No problem.

I asked my father why we were going to see this guy. He told me that Giovanni had done something wrong many years ago, and didn't deserve the punishment that had originally been prescribed for him.

Giovanni had to leave New York and re-locate to California, where he was now raising a family.

We headed out to the San Fernando Valley. It didn't take long to arrive in Giovanni's North Hollywood neighborhood.

I parked in front of the house, and went up and knocked on the door. My father was sitting in the car, watching me.

A woman came to the door and asked who I was and what I wanted. I asked her if her husband was named Giovanni. She told me yes. I introduced myself as Johnny Martino.

The woman turned around, and looked at her husband to see if he recognized the name. He was sitting on the couch, wearing sunglasses. Giovanni reminded me of the actor, Richard Conte.

He yelled out to his wife, asking who was at the door. She yelled back, and I also chimed in, dropping my father's name.

Giovanni literally jumped up from the couch and rushed towards the door. At this point, he wasn't sure if I was telling him the truth or not. I assured him that it was no joke, and told Giovanni that my father was sitting in the car.

'Your father is sitting in the car?'

'Yes, he's sitting in the car.'

By this time, Giovanni had opened the front door and was rapidly walking towards the car. My father got out and moved toward Giovanni. It was an amazing moment.

They embraced, and I heard Giovanni say, 'Thank you for saving me. I am so thankful that I can see you again.'

128

My father interrupted the hugs and introduced me. Giovanni was then hugging me. His wife came out, and we both received a lot more hugs. Another amazing moment!"

Johnny Martino does not know for sure why his father asked him to drive to Giovanni's house that day, but it was an event that helped move his acting career in Hollywood up a notch.

When Johnny first arrived in Hollywood, he went looking for work at Porcini's, another restaurant owned by Frank Sinatra and his manager, Hank Sinacola.

A young maître'd named Richard met him at the door. Johnny asked Richard for a job, but he replied that he didn't need any new help at the moment.

The day after he and his father arrived at Giovanni's house in North Hollywood, Johnny ran into Richard again. It turned out that he was Giovanni's son. Richard was definitely well connected to the Sinatra family and the entertainment world -- and his father owed Johnny's father a huge favor!

***

"It was a Sunday, and I was at this big party. Who is at the party? Richard. He is the son of my father's friend, the one whose life my father saved.

Richard did not know who I was at the time I was trying to get the job at Porcini's.

However, the day after I visited his father's home, he came over to me and said that I looked familiar. I asked him if he worked at a restaurant called Porcini's. He confirmed that he did. I told him that I had come to him awhile back asking for a job.

At this point, Richard put his arm around me and hugged me. He told me that he was so sorry. It would have been different had he known.

I told him that it was alright, and that I had a job working at the Villa Capri. However, he felt badly, knowing who my father was and how he had helped Richard's father. He could not apologize enough.

I told him not to worry. I had a job and I was happy. I told him that the only reason why I was in California was because I was trying to break into the movies as an actor. I told him that my father and mother had come out to visit me because they missed me.

I also assured Richard that I was glad I had gotten to see his family. I told him that now we could see each other, and that we were like relatives. We became good friends.

One day while visiting with Richard and his family, Giovanni told me that he wanted to reciprocate my father's favor and help me in any way that he could. He lived next door to a guy named Carlo, who worked at CBS Studio Center.

130

As Giovanni thought about it, he turned to me and said, 'Wait a minute.'

He then rushed next door and told his neighbor that he wanted him to meet a good friend from New York. Carlo, a bald-headed Italian, came over, and Giovanni introduced us.

Giovanni told Carlo that I needed a job and asked if maybe he could get me a little job in the studio. Carlo thought about it a moment, and said that maybe he could get me into the studio with a job in the labor department.

Carlo went to bat for me with the managers at the studio. Soon after, I was offered a union job as a laborer. I wasted no time in joining the union and reported to work at the studio.

I found myself one step closer to realizing my dream of becoming an actor in Hollywood. I was no longer working in restaurants and hoping for a break.

Now I was at CBS hoping for a break. It seemed one major step closer to that star I was reaching for. This happened about a year and a half after my father's visit to Giovanni."

21

THE WILD WILD WEST

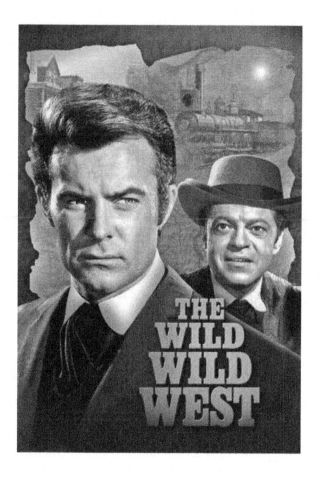

Johnny loved working on the various TV sets at CBS for shows such as *Get Smart*. When work at CBS slowed down, he found himself assigned to union jobs at Warner Brothers and

Samuel Goldwyn. It was the heyday for network television shows, and Johnny always found himself busy working on sets. Then he got his first acting break.

"I was at CBS and a popular western series called *The Wild Wild West* was filming. The script called for some underwater scenes, so we went out on location to Marineland, where the scenes could be shot through the aquarium glass.

We were all working long days on location -- from early morning until midnight.

One night, I was riding back to the studio in the same car with Mike Modor, the production manager. Mike was a really nice guy and very easy to talk to. So I asked him what I had to do to get my Screen Actors Guild card.

Mike told me that if I could get a little bit part, or something like that, then he could contact the union and make me eligible for membership. I told him that this would be great. Then I asked him how I could get a bit part.

Mike told me that the scripts came out every week, and that I needed to get a copy of a script from someone I knew on the lot. He told me to ask around, and find out when a suitable part became available. When I found a part that I could do, Mike told me to get back to him.

One of my co-workers in the labor department was a really nice guy who had done a lot of small roles. I was pretty sure that he knew quite a few people at the studio. I told him that

I had spoken with Mike Modor about doing a little part on *The Wild Wild West*, and he said that he would try to help me out.

Sure enough, he found a script which called for a Mexican guard. The part had a couple lines, including, 'Hey you. You don't belong around here!'

I wasted no time calling Mike Modor. I told him about the part I could do on *The Wild Wild West*, and asked him if this would get me into the union. He told me that it would work, and to come on up to his office.

At the time, I did not realize that the production manager was over everyone. Mike picked up the phone, and called the Screen Actors Guild. He told them, 'I have a new actor coming in -- Johnny Martino. We are going to sign him up. He has a role on *The Wild Wild West*.'

Mike hung up the phone and told me to go over to the Screen Actors Guild Office, pay my $215 initiation fee, and pick up my SAG card.

I was in. My acting career would begin on CBS television with a role in *The Wild Wild West*. I was living my dream and wishes beyond the stars were coming true.

Thank you, Mike Modor, for launching my acting career in Hollywood."

***

After his big moment in front of the cameras, Johnny soon found himself back at work in the CBS labor department.

"One day, I was working in the studio when one of the big shots asked me if I moved furniture also. I told him yes.

He told me that Mr. Gillette recently had his old office remodeled, and they needed to move some furniture. He asked me if I would do the job, and I told him yes.

This big shot told me to pick who I wanted to help me move the furniture.

There was no elevator, as I recall, so it was not going to be very easy. Plus, the furniture looked very expensive. It would need to be handled with care.

I decided the best method would be to carry the furniture up the wrought-iron steps on the side of the building and bring it into the office from the outside.

After expending a lot of sweat and elbow grease, I finished the job and released my helpers. The office looked fabulous, with all the expensive furniture placed in just the right spots.

Mr. Gillette, who turned out to be the president of CBS, was also very pleased with the look of his re-modeled office. He turned around and told the superintendent of the lot to ask me if I wanted to 'step up'.

I asked what that meant, and the superintendent told me that I could become an assistant superintendent. He told me that I would not punch a clock, but would work around the clock as an administrator. Basically whenever they needed me I would have to be there.

136

I asked him what the pay was, and he told me that I would get so much a week as a salary. Everything was really sounding great. Then I asked him if I would also have time to act. At that point, we arrived at the deal-breaker.

The superintendent told me that acting would not be possible because it would interfere with my regular steady job as an administrator. He told me not to worry about the acting, and to forget about it. I told him that I really wanted to do the acting, so I took a pass on the assistant superintendent job.

I knew that my options were limited at CBS now, because I refused the assistant superintendent job. It was time for me to leave the studio."

***

While still working at CBS, Johnny met an attractive secretary named Regan. Once again, he created an opportunity by doing a favor for someone. Regan had wanted a new desk from the warehouse, and Johnny did not hesitate to move it for her.

To return the favor, Regan introduced Johnny to her boss, who turned out to be producer Garry Marshall. Marshall was currently in production with a movie called *How Sweet It Is,* and suggested that Johnny might be able to land a small role. Marshall told Johnny he would be ideal for a small part playing a bartender.

The scene involved Debbie Reynolds and James Garner walking into a bar at the end of the movie. Debbie Reynolds would open her top to attract the bartender's attention. Marshall then asked Johnny if he would like the part.

"I told him I would definitely do it. It was a great part. I would love to do the scene. If you watch the movie and blink during my scene, you will miss my part. That's how quick the scene was.

That was okay with me, however, because it was a first for my acting career. I was now in a feature motion picture."

Soon, another project came Johnny's way. Director Jerry Parris was filming *The Grasshopper*, starring Jim Brown and Jacqueline Bisset.

Parris had come up through the ranks as an actor, working alongside stars like Ernest Borgnine in such movies as *Marty*. As a Hollywood director, Parris made his mark primarily in television, most notably on *Happy Days*.

This particular day in the late 1960's, however, Jerry Parris was making a movie, and he cast Johnny in a love scene with Jacqueline Bisset.

"I was to do the love scene in *The Grasshopper*, starring Jim Brown and Jacqueline Bisset.

138

She is supposed to be a hooker, and I go into the room to make out with her. Nudity was not a big thing during this time. They wanted her to do a little bit more. You know how Hollywood is. They want to get a little excitement going on.

I sat next to Jacqueline on the bed, and they told me to lay next to her. She did not want to take her top off, but when I got next to her, she flipped down her top.

I said to myself, 'Whoa, I don't even want to look.' Then they told me to get her top off. I started kissing her, kissing her, kissing her, and kissing her some more.

They told me that it was incredible. I finished the scene, and that was it.

I am so happy that they never actually showed the scene in the final cut. Jacqueline Bisset was much too classy for a scene like that."

22

THE GODFATHER

In Hollywood, networking is frequently the key to landing a break-through role. It was no different in Johnny Martino's case. One of his friends from *The Wild Wild West* days was a fellow actor named Eddie Reardon.

Eddie used the name Eddie Fontaine for his screen credits, and enjoyed a lot of success with recurring roles in such series as *The Gallant Men* and *The Rockford Files*.

About a year after Johnny found himself in bed kissing Jacqueline Bisset, Eddie Fontaine was on the phone.

"Eddie told me about a book called *The Godfather*. He had just read the book and really loved it. Eddie strongly recommended that I go out and buy it, which I did.

I only made it through the first few pages, when I realized that if Hollywood ever turned that book into a movie, the part of the main character -- Michael Corleone -- would be ideal for me.

As I read the book, I kept visualizing myself as Michael. No wonder Eddie recommended it to me. He saw the same thing.

In my mind, I played Michael throughout the entire book. I liked the others characters too. They were all interesting, but I was thinking, 'I'm Michael. That part was written for me. Michael was a young Italian kid. His father was the Don. Wow!'

Soon after reading the book, I learned that they were going to make the movie."

Johnny's next big break came from a rather unusual source – a Jewish doctor in Beverly Hills who had taken a liking to the struggling young actor seeking fame and fortune in Hollywood.

142

"I think Dr. Weiss was a diagnostician. He always had a cigarette hanging out of his mouth and would diagnose whatever you had. Doc Weiss liked me a lot. In fact, he introduced me to another famous doctor -- Dr. Siegel -- who was Marilyn Monroe's personal physician.

Shortly before New Year's 1970, Dr. Weiss told me that he was going to Al Martino's house for a New Year's Eve party, and asked if I wanted to come along.

Weiss told me that one of his friends -- Al Ruddy -- was going to be there. Then he dropped the big bombshell. *The Godfather* was going to be made into a movie and Al Ruddy was assigned as the producer."

Johnny wasted no time accepting the invitation. In 1970, Al Martino lived in a house in Beverly Hills on Rockford Drive.

Johnny made his way to the party, and immediately began to mix and mingle. He noticed actor James Caan in the crowd, and shared a few drinks and social conversation with him. Then Al Ruddy walked over and introduced himself.

"Everybody was having a good time. Al Ruddy asked me how I was doing, and he told me I had a nice look. I just might be right for *The Godfather* movie. I was thrilled. I already knew which part I wanted."

Ruddy told Johnny to keep in touch and call him occasionally, mentioning that he was working out of an office at Paramount.

Time went by and nothing happened. Rumors were flying around Hollywood. Maybe they were casting the movie, and maybe not.

A year passed, and still no word.

"It is now 1971 and I have not heard anything. There were rumors that the script was done, and they were starting to cast the movie. I also learned that Francis Ford Coppola was assigned as the director.

Finally, in March, 1971, I picked up the phone and called Paramount. When I asked for Al Ruddy, they told me he was in New York, and that he may have already started filming the movie. It did not look good for me."

However, persistence is one trait that Johnny never fails to use in pursuit of his dreams beyond the stars. Giving up was never an option.

"I asked the studio for Al Ruddy's number in New York, and I immediately gave him a call. Ruddy asked me how I was doing and where I was. I told him that I was in California, and he asked me for my number. This was back in the days before Caller ID.

Ruddy told me to stay by the phone and promised to call back in five minutes. Sure enough, five minutes later the phone rang.

'Get in your car and go directly to Paramount Studios. You'll be reading for the part of a character named Paulie Gatto, in Bob Evans' office,' said Ruddy.

Oh my God! Bob Evans was the president of Paramount!

Al stressed that I had to go immediately, that it was very important that I go right then, without a moment's delay. He ended the conversation by telling me that he would talk to me later.

I got into my car and drove over to Paramount Studios. I could feel the adrenaline pumping. I gave my name at the gate, and the guard let me right in. My heart was pounding. Can you believe it? My name was on the list to go right in.

I asked someone where Bob Evans' office was located, and found it with no difficulty whatsoever.

Fred Roos, the casting director for the movie, came walking into the office shortly after I arrived. We greeted each other, and then he told me about the scene that I would be reading. Fred told me to let him know when I was ready, and he would have someone come in and read with me.

Then Garry Marshall came walking in. He was a major producer at Paramount, with an office just down the hall from the president's office.

Garry was the person who Fred had asked to read with me. He would throw Clemenza's lines, while I did Paulie's lines.

I felt that I was really well prepared to bring Paulie Gatto to life for these major studio executives. I knew that this was the chance of a lifetime, the moment for which I had been training all these years. This could be my big break in Hollywood.

'Hey Rocco, sit on the other side, you block the rear view mirror,' I growled in my thick New York accent. After we ran through the entire scene, Garry Marshall felt I was ready. I thought so too.

I knocked on Bob Evans' door and he called for me to come in. After I finished with all of the lines in the scene, Evans told me that it was good. He asked me if I spoke Italian, and I answered back with something in Italian.

Then I received the standard closing comments heard at any audition. 'Thanks for coming in,' said the president of Paramount. 'We'll let you know.'

It was around 2:30 in the afternoon when I left the studio and started the drive back home. By 5 o'clock I had not heard anything. I began thinking that nothing was going to happen.

Then the moment I had been waiting for. The phone rang at about 5:30.

'May I speak to Johnny Martino please.'

146

'This is Johnny Martino.'

"I'm calling from Paramount Studios. Congratulations. You have the part of Paulie Gatto in *The Godfather*. You need to fly to New York this weekend because you begin filming on Monday. You'll be working a guaranteed three weeks at $750 per week.'

'Oh my God! Thank you so much. Thank you so much.'

That weekend, I flew home to New York as a cast member in Francis Ford Coppola's *The Godfather*."

***

No one knew back then that *The Godfather* was destined to become one of the most popular motion pictures of all time.

Johnny was thrilled because he had landed a role with some real substance to it, and he was working as a Hollywood actor on location in some of his old childhood neighborhoods in New York. That was all that mattered.

When the production people allowed him to drive his vintage 1940's coupe home one night, Johnny wasn't about to leave it parked.

He can't recall how many family members and friends ended up riding around Brooklyn in his death scene car, but the list was fairly extensive. Rumor has it that even some real-life wise guys took a ride in the death scene car.

Johnny was also having the time of his life on screen. Not content to blend into the background during the elaborate opening wedding scene, he decided to surreptitiously steal money from a woman's purse while cameras were rolling.

The director loved it. Months later, Marlon Brando paid Johnny the ultimate compliment, telling him that he had effortlessly stolen the entire scene with the purse-stealing incident.

Johnny regards his death scene, however, as the most exciting part of the entire experience on location. The director, Francis Ford Coppola, placed a real marksman in the back seat of the vintage 1941 coupe with a real .22 rifle and real ammunition. This caught Johnny's undivided attention.

It turned out that Johnny would have to be very precise in the way he moved, because the marksman in the back seat was set to put three bullet holes through the windshield at just the

148

right moment. Everything had to be perfect. There could only be one 'take.'

Coppola did not want to lose either the scene or the actor. In the end, everything went off as planned, and Johnny heard three bullets whiz by, clearing his head by inches. He slumped over and pulled the string attached to his hat. Paulie Gatto was dead – rubbed out as a traitor to the Corleone Family. Johnny Martino, the actor, was glad to still be alive!

"Richard Castellano, the three hundred pound actor who played Clemenza, was so large that the crew actually had to remove the car door so that he could get into the front seat with me.

Richard loved food, and he had a huge appetite on the set. It was fitting that he got the one famous line in the movie connected with food: 'Leave the gun and take the cannoli.'

Unfortunately, he passed away when he was only 58 years old.

In any event, we finished filming my death scene in the car on East 5th and Avenue S. I knew that they had not cast anyone yet to play the part of the singer -- Johnny Fontaine.

The next day, I approached Francis and suggested Al Martino. I had met Al a year prior to the film. He was such a nice guy. I socialized with him and his friends occasionally at his home in Beverly Hills. I knew that he really wanted the role.

A few days later, I was back at my mother's house late one night watching TV. Rona Barrett came on and announced that Al Martino just landed the part of Johnny Fontaine in *The Godfather* movie. I was thrilled.

The next day Al showed up in New York at his hotel. When I first suggested him to Francis, I didn't get a very enthusiastic response.

Francis didn't think Al had any acting ability. I assured him that Al had a great voice and could really come through for him. I told Francis I would be willing to coach Al with his lines before he went on the set. Apparently, Francis was willing to give Al Martino a chance. Meanwhile, I was about to become Al Martino's acting coach.

I worked with Al over the weekend, along with a friend of mine -- Tommy Signorelli (who was also an actor and appeared in quite a few films).

Between the two of us, we did a pretty good job of prepping Al for the role of Johnny Fontaine.

Al had never taken an acting lesson in his life. He was a professional singer. We had very little time to turn him into a professional actor.

On his first day on the set with Marlon Brando, Al was doing a really fine job with his lines. Marlon realized that Al was an inexperienced actor, however, so he just couldn't resist having a little fun at Al's expense.

150

The scene was proceeding as rehearsed -- when suddenly, Brando appeared to lose his temper and slapped Al hard across the face.

This was totally unexpected, and Al stood there in shock. Robert Duvall was sitting there too. We kind of laughed in the background, but the scene worked, and it turned out looking fantastic on screen. When you watch that particular moment in the film the next time, remember that Al Martino never saw that slap coming – and Marlon delivered a pretty vigorous slap!.

I was really happy that Al got his chance to be in *The Godfather*. It was a great example of Italians helping each other. I was able to put my two cents in with the director, and he was willing to give Al a chance. Al always made it a point to express his appreciation whenever I went to see him sing. He would always say, 'Ladies and Gentleman...Johnny Martino. A great friend, and if it weren't for Johnny, I probably wouldn't have been in *The Godfather* movie.'

People always thought that Al and I were related because we had the same last name. However, Martino was his stage name, not his real name. For me, it was a thrill to work in a movie with Al Martino. He was a nice guy and I enjoyed all of his music when I was growing up.

One night during the filming of the movie, we did a celebrity appearance at a benefit event in Long Island. I took Al with me and my mother and brothers. Over the years, I became

151

very close to Al Martino and his beautiful wife Judy. They were great people."

***

In Hollywood, a movie goes through several stages before it is finally ready for distribution to the theatres. Once filming has been completed, the project moves to the post-production phase. Editors go to work piecing all of the shots together in a way which will tell an entertaining story. Sound effects and music are added, along with special visual effects.

Frequently, actors are called back in to the studio to record their lines under perfect conditions, free of any background noise. This process is called looping.

Soon after filming was completed, Paramount contacted Johnny and asked him to fly to New York to loop his lines. Al Pacino, Robert Duvall, and Richard Castellano would join him in the sound studio that day, and loop their lines as well. It was a nice little re-union for the actors portraying the Corleone Family.

Then it was New Year's Eve, 1971.

23

MARLON BRANDO

"I got a call from Francis Ford Coppola telling me to come to Paramount Studios to do some looping. He mentioned that Marlon Brando would be there that day also.

I arrived at Paramount and went directly into the sound studio. Marlon came in earlier and was in the process of looping some of his lines. Once he finished a particular piece of dialogue, I joined him in front of the microphone. Francis Ford Coppola was with us also.

Francis told me to do my lines again from the wedding purse scene. He told me to use a 'New York accent,' but not too much.

After I finished my lines, Marlon got up and walked over to me.

'That was really good. I like you very much,' he said in his young Marlon Brando voice (not his Don Corleone voice).

This was great. Here was my idol standing next to me, complimenting my work.

Suddenly, Marlon grabbed me with two hands and kissed me on both sides of my face.

After about three hours of looping, Francis told me that he knew that I sang in Italian. He asked me to give him a few lines of any song that I liked -- in Italian.

When I finished singing, Marlon was so impressed that he came over and gave me a big hug and a kiss again. He told me that the song was amazing, and he asked me if I could teach him to speak Italian. I told him sure.

Before long, Marlon was telling me stories about himself. One time, he was in the Orient doing a movie. I believe it was *Tea House in the August Moon.*

154

One night he really got plastered. He remembered that he got drunk, but he couldn't remember anything else. He spent most of the night out cold.

Suddenly, he opened his eyes, moved his head a bit and saw thousands of different things. He was too scared to move.

I asked him what he thought it was.

Marlon replied, 'Things started to move on my face again and I really began to panic. Then I discovered what it was.'

I listened intently.

'It was an Oriental girl with long hair wrapped around my face. I was in bed with her, and her hair was all over my face. Every time it moved, I didn't know what it was.'

Marlon told me that he was so drunk that the girl had taken him to her apartment and placed him in bed with her. He did not know what was happening at any time, and it was pretty frightening when he first started to gain consciousness. All he knew at first was that something seemed to be crawling across his face.

He and I began to laugh really hard. Here I was, talking to my movie idol, Marlon Brando, and it was beautiful.

Since one good story deserved another, I decided to tell Marlon about my year in Italy with Lucky Luciano, which he found fascinating.

Then Marlon announced that it was New Year's Eve and he had champagne coming. Almost immediately, someone brought in a bottle of champagne.

Marlon Brando went to open up the bottle, and then paused.

'Do me a favor and look the other way for a minute.'

I looked the other way.

'Do you have a quarter?'

I reached into my pocket and gave Marlon a quarter.

'I'll be with you in a minute.'

Out of the corner of my eye, I could see that he was shaping something with the foil that had been wrapped around the cork and neck of the bottle.

When he finished, I turned around. He had made a tiny champagne glass with the foil. It was a perfectly shaped champagne glass, complete with the stem and a base made from my quarter.

Marlon handed me the little glass that he made and poured the champagne into it.

'Salud,' said Marlon Brando.

I took a sip from the tiny foil glass and then I gave it back to Marlon. He took a sip. We both drank champagne out of the little glass that Marlon Brando had fashioned from the foil. It never leaked once.

We finally finished up the looping and the champagne, and Marlon said, 'John, I enjoyed working with you today. It's New Year's. How about you spend the day with me? We'll go out tonight and have a great time on the town.'

I said, 'Wow, I would love that, but some friends have invited me over, and I don't want to disappoint them. We could definitely do it another time.'

Marlon repeated that he enjoyed being with me that day. He told me that he did not get to know me on the set, but that it was nice meeting me in the looping studio.

That was a special day for me – being with Marlon Brando. However, when I left the studio, I forgot the little glass that he made for me. Even to this day I say to myself, 'What a moment!

I may not have the little foil glass today, but I do have some great memories of being in the presence of someone else who wished beyond the stars, and found his wishes all coming true.

That New Year's Eve will never be forgotten."

***

"One day I was at Warner Brothers, and Frank Sinatra was on the lot. Someone told me, 'Frankie's on the stage.' At the time, he was negotiating with Jack Warner to buy Warner Brothers studios.

Frankie somehow talked Jack Warner into selling the studio (money talks, and Frank had it), because shortly after that meeting, the company changed its name to Warner Brothers/Seven Arts. I believe owning the studio was one of

157

Frank Sinatra's dreams beyond the stars, and things turned out great for him too.

Shortly before I was cast in *The Godfather*, Frankie expressed some mixed feelings about the film project. However, he told me that if I could get a part in it, I should go ahead and do it.

Frankie felt that *The Godfather* had the potential of being a great movie, and he knew that it was going to be made regardless of how he felt about it. I believe that once Frankie did see the movie when it finally came out, he enjoyed it. And it did become a legendary film.

Frankie probably would have loved to play the role of Godfather Don Corleone, and he could have done a great job. Of course, Brando got the part and Sinatra did not.

I do know that Marlon researched the part extensively by traveling incognito to a neighborhood park and observing the elderly men gathered there. He noted how they shuffled when they walked, how they stooped over, and how they sometimes talked breathlessly, slowly, deliberately.

When Marlon arrived at the studio for his screen test, he came in full make-up. He had the cotton stuffed in his mouth, the wrinkles, the nose putty – everything.

When a studio executive spotted the screen test on a monitor, he asked who it was. Marlon was totally unrecognizable. That day, he was Don Corleone, and he looked, acted, and breathed the part in every way. I just don't think

Frankie would have gone to such lengths to nail the role. Marlon knew what he had to do.

Today, we all love and respect Brando's brilliant performance in the movie, and I can't imagine anyone else portraying Don Corleone.

God bless Marlon Brando. He was one-of-kind, and a legend in his own time."

***

In 2005, Johnny Martino flew to Omaha, Nebraska with Marlon's son Miko. Despite the various international locations Marlon periodically identified to reporters as his birthplace, the fact of the matter is that he came from Omaha -- not Singapore, Buenos Aires or anywhere else.

Johnny and Miko were scheduled to appear at a fund-raising event to benefit deaf and hard-of-hearing children in Marlon's home-town.

According to the event promoters, the night was a sell-out and produced a record amount of charitable contributions – well over $120,000 -- none of which (according to Johnny) went to the Corleone family!

During the screening of *The Godfather*, Johnny noticed that Miko was looking upset. He had not seen the film since his father's death, which turned out to be very similar to Marlon's death scene in the movie.

Johnny reassured him, and they were both able to stay until the end of the film.

24

MY WAY

"One of my favorite Sinatra songs of all time was actually written and performed first by a singer named Paul Anka. One of Sinatra's friends who doubled as his personal bodyguard – a guy named Jilly Rizzo – heard Paul sing the song one night at a club appearance. When Anka spotted Jilly in the audience, he waved him over after the show.

'Can you please tell Frank that I wrote a song and I think that it would be great for him?' Paul asked. Jilly said he would see what he could do.

By the time he reported back to Sinatra, Jilly was really enthusiastic about the song, and he persuaded Frank to take the time to go see Paul performing it.

Paul arranged a private audition of the song for Frank at a place where they had access to a piano. When Paul had finished singing and playing the song, Frankie was absolutely amazed. He turned around and told Paul to write the song up for him. He liked it a lot.

The next thing you know -- it was maybe weeks later -- the arrangements were completed and Frank Sinatra was in a studio recording *My Way*.

Of course, it became such a very powerful song for Frank Sinatra, especially at a time late in life where he could look back and truly say that he had done everything his way."

It turns out that Paul Anka and Frank Sinatra were not the only recording artists passionate about *My Way*. The singer who recorded *Babysitting Baby* regards *My Way* as his signature song as well.

"I adore the song. I absolutely love it, and managed to also record it. I even like doing it a cappella. I will sing it the way that I feel in my heart, the way that I felt about it when Sinatra recorded it. It is a very powerful song."

162

25

DILLINGER & CAPONE

In 1972, Johnny found himself in demand in Hollywood. When director John Milieus' office called, asking if he would be interested in a role in an upcoming movie starring Warren Oates,

Johnny did not hesitate. He made a beeline to Milieus' office, where a secretary asked him to have a seat.

After waiting ten minutes, Johnny could wait no longer. He got up and knocked on the famous director's door, and then let himself in.

"Milieus immediately recognized me from *The Godfather,* and invited me to come in and sit down. He then introduced me to Steve Canales and Richard Dreyfuss, who were also meeting with him.

Milieus told me that the movie was called *Dillinger,* and I could have the role of Eddie Shouse, John Dillinger's real-life driver. I accepted it on the spot."

The production company offered Johnny $3,000 a week for two weeks of work on location in Enid, Oklahoma.

However, the producers discovered that the real Eddie Shouse -- a mob mechanic working out of Chicago before teaming up with Dillinger -- was still alive.

To avoid paying out any life rights, they changed the name of Johnny's character to Eddie Martin.

***

"One of my favorite actors is Ben Johnson. I loved the role he played in *Shane.* He was Warren Oates' co-star in Dillinger, so we had opportunities to sit and chat while filming in Enid.

164

In the car one day, I asked him how he liked working with Alan Ladd in *Shane*. He told me that Alan was a really short actor with powerful looks and a great voice.

Ben said that Alan was great to work with, and he thoroughly enjoyed the entire experience, being that he was a real-life cowboy off-screen. It turned out that Ben Johnson owned a beautiful ranch, complete with horses and cattle."

Although they were friendly off-camera, on-screen Ben Johnson and Johnny Martino were mortal enemies. In the end, Johnny dies in a hail of machine-gun fire.

In the longest death scene ever recorded on film up to that time, Johnny reacts to twenty-seven explosive squibs going off all over his body before he falls dead to the ground. He managed to do it all in one take. John Milieus instantly awarded him a $2500 bonus.

A year later, Johnny received a call from a producer's representative, asking if he would be interested in a role in a film called *Capone,* which would star veteran actor Ben Gazzara and newcomer Sylvester Stallone.

"They offered me $750 for a day's work. I knew this would be another period piece, and my hair had just grown back from *Dillinger.* So I passed on this one.

It wasn't long and the phone rang again. If I would cut my hair, they would pay $1500 for the day. I immediately accepted, and was assigned a great scene with Ben Gazzara at the end of the movie.

In between takes, I had an opportunity to visit with Sly Stallone, who was still struggling to break into the business. As I recall, he lived in a little apartment on Balboa at the time.

Sly asked me what I was doing on the side and I told him I was writing a screenplay about a down-and-out boxer who falls in love with his neighborhood sweet-heart, and – against all odds – this boxer makes a spectacular come-back. I told him the title of my screenplay was *The Winner Is.*

'You think that would sell?" Sly asked me.

I told him I thought it had great potential, and listed a dozen boxing movies, many of which were break-through films for the lead actors. Sly was definitely listening."

Shortly after filming wrapped up on *Capone*, Johnny heard through the grapevine that Stallone had written an outline with a boxer/love story motif, and floated it around the studios. No one wanted it.

However, Stallone's own wish beyond the stars was about to come true. He came across a couple of independent producers who believed in the project, mortgaged their homes to the hilt, and gambled everything on the movie. *Rocky* would not let them down.

"I like to think that I inspired Sly to write his breakthrough movie. I just knew the time was ripe for another love story about a boxer."

26

A WISH BEYOND THE STARS

Johnny Martino is at a stage of his life where he can look back and say that much of what he has accomplished was done his way.

Like many aspiring actors, Johnny arrived in Hollywood and went to work in a restaurant. Those restaurant days were far from boring, however.

It is not every day that you get to bump into Marilyn Monroe, or serve cappuccino to the next President of the United States. Johnny may be the only person alive to have given Marlon Brando a quarter, and received a hand-made foil wine glass in return.

Johnny's charismatic personality opened many doors in Hollywood, and he found himself cast in major roles with major stars in major motion pictures.

Johnny believes that God still has a purpose for his life, and he has lots more to do before reporting to that multi-screen cinema in the sky.

"There are many little children in the world who are living in abject poverty. They wake up each day to hunger and deprivation. There is no one to love them, hug them, or kiss them.

169

I believe God is telling me that I have to help them. I have often wondered what I could do. Then I remembered the time when I was in Italy in 1947. There were children walking around barefoot.

I said to myself that these children are starving and struggling to survive with no shoes on their feet.

Then it came to me. If I could just go around and put shoes on all of the barefooted children in the world, it would be a contribution beyond all contributions.

I actually started fulfilling this dream back in 1947 when we were in Italy with Lucky Luciano. I came across a poor, struggling barefooted kid in the street and I took my shoes off and gave them to him.

When I arrived back home, my mother asked me where my shoes were. I told her I just could not leave that kid walking around without any shoes. Besides, I had lots more in my closet.

My brother Charlie thought I was crazy, but my mother seemed to understand and approve.

On that day, I thought about reaching out and helping poor children all around the world. Someone needs to put shoes on their feet. It's my wish beyond the stars."

27

THE REST OF THE STORY

Documenting Johnny Martino's personal story was a real delight. Over several days of recorded interviews, Johnny spilled out an incredible number of details -- all in chronological order. He recalled names and events from a childhood that occurred more than 60 years in the past. Those memories are now safely preserved in this book, as well as in his incredible memory bank.

Fleshing out the story with details about Lucky Luciano was a bit more challenging. Even to this day, the war-time service Luciano provided to Naval Intelligence remains controversial and not easily accessible.

Was his contribution substantial or not? Was he pardoned from prison because of this secret service, or was his release due to a massive Mafia bribe? All sorts of versions exist in print and on the internet.

What about his activities with his childhood friend from Sicily – Gaetano Martino? What exactly did Gaetano do to assist Lucky in the secret government intelligence operation? He certainly didn't come home each night and share details with his family.

Yet for some inexplicable reason, after his testimony before the Kefauver Committee hearings in 1951, Gaetano

Martino was granted a highly confidential pardon for any illegal activity he may have been involved with up until that time. Why would the government ever do such a thing?

We know that the two most trusted friends Lucky Luciano had were Frank Costello and Gaetano Martino. Frank was the public figure who ran the mob while Lucky was in prison. Gaetano was the shadowy figure behind the scenes, outside of the public eye. I believe it was Gaetano Martino who carried out Lucky Luciano's intelligence plans -- plans which were developed in collaboration with United States Naval Intelligence.

So when Meyer Lansky and Frank Costello visited Lucky Luciano in prison, carrying a plea from U.S Naval Intelligence to help make the New York docks safe from Nazi espionage and sabotage, Lucky reached out to his childhood friend – Gaetano Martino, who was a powerful dock superintendent ruling over the New York waterfront.

Since Lucky was in prison, he needed someone he could trust to facilitate his plans to assist the government. Gaetano Martino and Frank Costello were the only choices available to him. Frank was busy running the mob.

Gaetano was in the right place as a superintendent on the waterfront. While he never discussed business with his family, Gaetano Martino had to have been up to his neck in Luciano's war-time service to America. If this were the case, it now makes sense that the Kefauver Committee would arrange a pardon, once they realized the extent of the Luciano-Martino connection.

However, the story takes an incredible turn in 1942, about the time Lucky Luciano decides to remain in prison to help with the Allied invasion of Sicily.

At this time, Gaetano Martino resigned his very lucrative job on the waterfront, and quietly joined the U.S. Merchant Marine. Disguised as a black marketeer, he made a dozen trips to enemy-held Sicily, transporting cigarettes and penicillin. No one but his family and the government knew he was in the Merchant Marine. Even his family did not know why he gave up his position on the waterfront.

Yet his experiences were right out of a James Bond novel. He told his son, Johnny, about one incident where he had to travel inland on a horse-drawn cart. He sensed danger, knocked the driver off the cart, and escaped to a safe house, but not before gunfire erupted. After all, he was an American in Mussolini's Fascist Italy during a time of war.

Because of the secret nature of his work, Gaetano never mentioned his Merchant Marine service in public, referring only to his army service in World War I.

In 1951, the Luciano intelligence operation was still shrouded in government secrecy, so even the Kefauver Committee did not hear of the Merchant Marine connection – at least not in public.

When things are kept secret, rumors start to develop. By 1954, rumors were flying that Lucky Luciano bought his pardon with a $250,000 Mafia bribe. Alarmed at the potential damage these rumors could cause to his reputation, Thomas E. Dewey decided it was time to publicly share the truth – even if it meant painting his underworld nemesis as a white knight.

So Dewey reached out to attorney William B. Herlands, who was the New York Commissioner of Investigations. He tasked Herlands with documenting Lucky Luciano's involvement with the eastern seaboard security operation.

Herlands produced a document of 2,993 pages, from which he concluded, "The evidence demonstrates that Luciano's assistance and cooperation was secured by Naval Intelligence in the cause of developing requirements of national security."

Popular columnist and radio commentator Walter Winchell went much further:

174

"For his work in connection with the defense of New York and the successful invasion of Sicily, Lucky Luciano should be nominated for the Congressional Medal of Honor."

Time Magazine was not far behind. It named Lucky Luciano one of the Top 100 people of the 20th century. His life-long childhood friend from Sicily -- Gaetano Martino – was always in the shadows by his side.

In 1947, as Gaetano Martino drove Lucky Luciano to the ship which would return him to Sicily, the two friends must have swapped their war-time stories about exploits that not only helped America in a time of peril, but also inevitably led to Luciano's successful release from prison.

That night, a number of well-dressed men in suits boarded the ship. They all carried fisherman's union cards, which allowed them to board.

They dined on spaghetti, lobster, and fine wine in a grand send-off for Lucky Luciano.

When Gaetano returned home that night, there were most likely tears in his eyes.

ABOUT THE AUTHOR

Richard Lester is the author of the best-selling books *Flight of The Blue Heron* and *Hollywood Legend: The Johnny Duncan Story.*

He is also a free-lance magazine writer, with published articles in *True Detective, American Legion, Florida Media Quarterly,* and *Mysteries Magazine.*

Lester has had a variety of career experiences, including high school teacher, community college instructor, national park ranger, radio & television broadcaster, and actor.

Lester's first film role was in the 1985 epic western, *Silverado,* directed by Lawrence Kasdan. He is a member of Screen Actor's Guild and the American Federation of Television & Radio Artists.

In 2005, Lester formed Blue Heron International Pictures, and – with his son, Gary – has produced a number of award-winning documentaries, including *Safe Haven: The Warsaw Zoo* and *The Weatherwax Legacy.*

Additional information is available at (www.blueheronpix.com)

CPSIA information can be obtained
at www.ICGtesting.com
Printed in the USA
BVOW09s1950121117

500214BV00019B/341/P